Spenser's Art

A Companion to Book One
of The Faerie Queene

Mark Rose

Harvard University Press
Cambridge, Massachusetts
London, England

All rights reserved
Second printing 1976
Publication of this book has been aided by a grant
from the Hyder Edward Rollins Fund

Library of Congress Catalog Card Number 74-21229
ISBN 0-674- 83193-4

Printed in the United States of America

Preface

More and more we have come to appreciate Spenser's stature as a writer of the first magnitude. Book One of *The Faerie Queene* is now regularly taught in colleges and universities not only in advanced courses for students particularly interested in Spenser or in the English Renaissance but also in introductory surveys for freshmen and sophomores. Spenser is a difficult poet. This short book was undertaken on the assumption that many readers feel less than wholly at ease with *The Faerie Queene.*

Allegory creates a stumbling block for many. After all, what is there to do with an allegory other than to explicate its meaning by translating it into abstract terms: the Christian soul becomes lost in the Wood of Error but with the help of Truth saves itself. Perhaps one can get some sort of debate going about whether Lucifera and Orgoglio represent exactly the same sort of Pride, but the exercise seems sterile and unsatisfying. An alternative—rarely adopted these days, I suspect—is to follow Hazlitt's advice and not meddle with the allegory, dwelling instead upon the lush beauties of Spenser's verse. But this, too, in its own way seems sterile.

Then there is the awkward business of religion. "The Legende of the Knight of the Red Crosse, or of Holinesse" is pretty clearly a religious poem. Many of us, embarrassed at our ignorance and intimidated by religion of any kind, assume that to understand *The Faerie Queene* one must have memorized the Bible and be familiar with obscure theological doctrines—an assumption that some of the critical literature has done much to reinforce. Nothing is quite so effective as the deadly specter of theology to convince the average freshman or sophomore, who already doubts his competence to read Spenser, that the whole enterprise is hopeless. And, as if theology were not a sufficient bugaboo, some have also heard the frightening rumor that *The Faerie Queene* is a complex historical allegory.

One obstacle, potentially the greatest of them all, no longer obstructs us. We are no longer inclined to dismiss romance as silly. The last decade or so has seen a major shift in literary taste that has made it possible for serious readers to enjoy such books as *The Lord of the Rings* and science-fiction novels such as Ursula Le Guin's *Left Hand of Darkness* or Frank Herbert's *Dune*. On a more exalted plane, the recent revival of interest in Shakespeare's late romances, *The Winter's Tale* and *The Tempest*, bears witness to the same change in taste. Most people have a healthy love of wonder and melodrama, but for many years the accepted canons of taste rejected the basic stuff of romance as childish. In the past, readers of *The Faerie Queene* could always justify their delight in a story about a hero and a dragon on solemn moral or antiquarian grounds, but now it may not seem necessary to explain such a pleasure away. The impulse to melodrama and romance, the natural human tendency to divide the world into heroes and villains, is perilous in life, but it can be an excellent foundation for art. The indispensable prerequisite for enjoying *The Faerie Queene* is an unembarrassed love of romance.

Of course there are romances and romances. *Dune* also satisfies a taste for the marvelous. But Spenser uses the conventions of romance to create a world that is in no sense simplistic. Like Shakespeare, with whom he has much more in common than most people realize, Spenser is ultimately great because his vision of life is so rich that it is always relevant to the fundamental humane task of knowing ourselves better. Enjoying a poem is one thing, understanding it another. The prerequisite for understanding *The Faerie Queene* is not knowledge of theology or history but some knowlege of people based upon experience. It is useful to understand the doctrine of original sin or to know who Henry VIII was, but it is much more important to know from personal experience the sad destructiveness of anger and the danger of casting oneself always in the role of righteous hero, to know that pretentious shows of well-being often disguise empty misery, or to understand how readily one can be in love with a fantasy of one's own making rather than with the real person who shares one's life.

To modern eyes *The Faerie Queene* appears somewhat chaotic. Spenser's flowing verse, formulaic repetitions of phrases, interjected comments in his own voice, episodic narrative technique, apparent digressions, and extended descriptions that seem to go on until the poet runs out of material—all these give the impression of looseness. Many people probably assume that since the poem appears to be loosely composed it can be read loosely. We look to Spenser for large effects and not—as we look to, say, Vergil or Dante—for precision, purpose, and complexity in the most minute details. Vergil, too, can be read for large effects alone, and in translation of course there is hardly any other way to read him. But I think most would agree that the closer one examines the *Aeneid* the more fascinating it becomes: every detail reveals thought.

Spenser conceived his poem as an epic and Vergil was one of his models. The first lines of the proem ("Lo I the man . . .") imitate Vergil's introductory verses, and the opening description of the "Gentle Knight" clad in "mightie armes" probably alludes to Vergil's opening "Arms and the man I sing." Indeed, Book One of *The Faerie Queene* is in a sense an extended allusion to the *Aeneid* and to the whole epic tradition, as the *Aeneid* itself is an extended allusion to Homer. To us Spenser seems a loose writer partially because we are unaccustomed to certain aspects of his technique and partially because he himself, living in a culture that valued graceful performance very highly, seeks to give an impression of fluid ease. Nevertheless, every detail in Spenser, as in Vergil, reveals purpose. The most satisfying way to read *The Faerie Queene* is to read it slowly and closely, and then read it again.

I have tried to suggest something of Spenser's richness and subtlety through a reading of Book One, following the poem as it develops canto by canto. In general, I have attempted to draw the meaning out of the text, emphasizing that the poem creates its own world of allusion, becoming increasingly suggestive as it proceeds. There are many aspects of the poem, important aspects such as the historical allegory, that I have ignored or slighted. My intention has not been to provide a complete study of Book One, but merely to indicate to the reader who does not come to Spenser equipped with special expertise how much he may gain through a study of the text itself.

On the assumption that most readers will find a short book more useful than a long one, I have tried to keep my discussions as brief as possible. Necessarily this has meant being selective about which passages and details to comment upon, and in a poem such as *The Faerie Queene* in which every detail is significant any selection is to some degree a distortion of the text. The reader should recognize this at the outset, realizing that another critic's choices of passages for emphasis might be quite different from my own.

This is not a book for specialists and, although I have appended a selected bibliography, I have with some qualms dispensed with the usual apparatus of annotation. Nevertheless, my thanks are due to Oxford University Press for permission to quote from *Spenser's Faerie Queene*, ed. J. C. Smith, 2 vols. (Oxford: The Clarendon Press, 1961), which is the edition I have used, normalizing certain aspects of the text such as the use of *u* for *v* and *i* for *j*. More important, I have felt free to make use of the learning and insight of many scholars, and conscience as well as gratitude compels me to mention at least the names of a few. Of special significance were the critical writings of Paul Alpers, Judith Anderson, Harry Berger, Donald Cheney, A. C. Hamilton, and Kathleen Williams, and I have also profited from Robert Kellogg's and Oliver Steele's annotated text edition of Books One and Two. My friends Max Byrd and Stephen Barney made many helpful suggestions, and I am grateful to Stephen for allowing me to read his work in progress on allegory. I am particularly indebted to A. C. Hamilton, who volunteered to read the manuscript and provided me with an invaluable list of comments and suggestions.

Contents

Spenser's Art

Like the opening of a film in which the camera focuses on the hero's face so that we may read his character in his physiognomy, or on some symbolic action in which the essence of the plot is implicit, *The Faerie Queene* opens with a powerfully isolated visual image for our contemplation, the picture of the anonymous knight riding along a plain.

> A Gentle Knight was pricking on the plaine,
>   Y cladd in mightie armes and silver shielde,
>   Wherein old dints of deepe wounds did remaine,
>   The cruell markes of many a bloudy fielde;
>   Yet armes till that time did he never wield:
>   His angry steede did chide his foming bitt,
>   As much disdaining to the curbe to yield:
>   Full jolly knight he seemd, and faire did sitt,
> As one for knightly giusts and fierce encounters fitt.
>   (i.1)

In film the camera directs our contemplation by dwelling upon details in sequence; Spenser's language shapes our response to his image in a similarly progressive fashion. The stanza's first lines describe the knight's mighty armor: our initial impression is of a perfected knight, strong and experienced. The fifth line—"Yet armes till that time did he never wield"—comes as a shock, forcing us to dismantle our image of the knight and distinguish between the arms and the man: the arms are mighty, the man unproved. The sixth and seventh lines, focusing on the steed foaming at the bit, reinforce our sense of the man's inexperience—he is having trouble with his horse—and simultaneously provide an image of heroic spiritedness. In the stanza's final lines Spenser returns to the opening picture of the knight, but now his language is more tentative, saying only that he seems a "jolly" knight—that is, "goodly"—and fit for battle. The language emphasizes that we are seeing the knight from the outside, that we must recognize the limits of our vision and the fact that at this point we can tell only what the man seems, not what, beneath his impressive armor, he is.

The first stanza, then, provides not only an opening picture but an experience in which an image is evoked, analyzed, and revalued. The revaluation, of course, does not cancel our original image of a complete, perfected knight. On the contrary, this first vision remains with us throughout the poem as the primal image of Book One and the standard against which everything else is measured. Nevertheless, the point of the opening stanza is the implicit lesson in our own limitations and the need to be wary of jumping to conclusions about the ultimate nature of things. This is a lesson that will be repeated as the poem proceeds, for in a sense it is *the* lesson of Book One: this is what the knight, through his experiences, will learn, and what we, through our experiences in reading the poem, will also learn.

The second stanza continues the description of the knight:

But on his brest a bloudie Crosse he bore,
    The deare remembrance of his dying Lord,
    For whose sweete sake that glorious badge he wore,

And dead as living ever him ador'd:
Upon his shield the like was also scor'd,
For soveraine hope, which in his helpe he had:
Right faithfull true he was in deede and word,
But of his cheere did seeme too solemne sad;
Yet nothing did he dread, but ever was ydrad.   (i.2)

Having followed the course of stanza 1 to its less than firm conclusion, we can respond to the cross on the knight's breast as a kind of reassurance, a significant qualification of the first stanza's final lines. This second stanza is in fact a series of qualifications, progressive complications of our understanding of the knight. The first seven lines insisting upon the knight's faithfulness lead to the suggestion in line 8 that a faithful knight should not look so "solemne sad." Why should a "sad" appearance—the word means both "grave" and "unhappy" here—be incompatible with faith? The implicit question is left unanswered as Spenser hurries on to reassure us that, nevertheless, the knight is fearless: "Yet nothing did he dread, but ever was ydrad." But this final qualification is double-edged because "yet" also means "up to this point," and even as the line asserts the knight's fearlessness it implies that this may be a function of his inexperience, that he has not yet discovered that there are things to be dreaded.

My purpose in scrutinizing the first two stanzas in this manner is to suggest how Spenser's technique is both visual and verbal. These stanzas do evoke a mental picture of an armored knight, emblazoned with the cross, riding a proud charger—a picture, even before the introduction of the lady with the lamb in the fourth stanza, reminiscent of manuscript images of St. George. But even as Spenser sketches this picture, his language is hard at work in specifically verbal ways. In order to understand Spenser, to experience the poem, we gradually realize that we have to see and listen at the same time—and this, as we shall discover, is also one of the things the knight has to learn as he gradually comes to appreciate the power of words.

The opening picture is completed with the description of the beautiful lady, a study in the black of mourning and the white of innocence, who in her humility is meant to be contrasted with the proud knight at her side and the lagging dwarf, already a somewhat comic figure. The lady's sadness—notice that Spenser explains why she is unhappy—contrasts with the knight's sadness, which is more mysterious because it is not explained, and the emphasis upon her innocence also points back to the knight who is, in a different sense of the word, equally innocent.

The first five stanzas introduce us to Spenser's normal poetic method in which the stanza is the basic unit of thought as well as versification. Spenser's stanzas generally reveal internal coherence, and when the narrative takes a new turn—as with the introduction of the lady in stanza 4—it often does so at the beginning of a stanza. Stanza 6 begins by introducing the dwarf—''Behind her farre away a Dwarfe did lag''—and the poem's established rhythm naturally leads us to expect that the entire stanza will be devoted to his description. It comes as something of a surprise when the description concludes in the middle of the stanza, indeed in the middle of a

line, and the action proper of Book One abruptly
begins:

> . . . Thus as they past,
> The day with cloudes was suddeine overcast,
> And angry Jove an hideous storme of raine
> Did poure into his Lemans lap so fast,
> That every wight to shrowd it did constrain,
> And this faire couple eke to shroud themselves were
> fain.   (i.6)

Spenser has organized his material so that the storm
occurs with the same suddenness for us as for the knight
and lady. Moreover, the language, especially the adjec-
tives in "angry Jove" and "hideous storme," makes us
perceive the storm from the characters' point of view,
responding to it as a threat and sympathizing with their
eagerness to take cover. Yet, even as we regard the storm
in this way, we should notice that it is into his leman's,
his beloved's, lap that the king of heaven is pouring his
waters. The image, which is common in classical literature, implies a divine sexual act with traditionally bene-
ficent connotations, the impregnation of mother earth
with life-giving water. The knight and lady, however,
like children ignorant of the sexual act, perceive the
heavenly father as angry when in fact he is loving.

The double perspective in which we regard the action
simultaneously from the characters' subjective point of
view and from a wider, more absolute and objective,
point of view continues in stanza 7 as we follow the
knight and lady into the shady grove that promises aid
and yet, ominously, comes between them and heaven's
light. At the start of the stanza the grove seems small—

"grove" does not imply a wood of any great extent—
but soon, as Spenser describes the paths and alleys
"leading inward farre," it begins to reveal itself as a
labyrinthine forest: "shadie grove," we realize, represents the way the knight and lady perceive what might
from another point of view be called a dark forest, an
image of danger and confusion with rich literary associations, recalling among other things the dark wood in
which Dante finds himself at the start of the *Inferno*.
"Faire harbour that them seemes," Spenser says, punning on "arbor" and "harbor," and then, with an un-
derstatement devastating in its simplicity: "so in they
entred arre."

In stanzas 6 and 7 Spenser has described the knight
and lady's initiation into a dark and potentially dangerous world. It would be a mistake, a serious violation of
the poem, to specify at this point what the forest
"means," translating Spenser's suggestive image into a
concept such as "theological error." We would not
think of substituting a reductive label of this sort for,
say, the dark forest in *A Midsummer Night's Dream*,
and reading Spenser requires the same kind of critical
tact. What we should notice is the subtlety with which
Spenser suggests the process of intellectual error, the
misconstruing of both the storm and the grove. And
now, in stanza 8, we should notice how, the knight and
lady having entered the wood, the tense shifts, significantly, into the passive, the couple being led by forest
pleasures deep into the labyrinth, joying in the singing
birds that seem to them to scorn what they still call the
"cruell sky."

Like the birds, the man and woman begin in effect to sing as they praise the majesty and use of the various trees. Moreover, like the birds, their song scorns heaven, for it seems to imply that the natural world is sufficient for human needs. Nevertheless, as the catalogue of woody virtues continues, we too get caught up in the song until, like the knight and lady, we can no longer see the forest for the trees: we too are becoming lost in nature until, in the final line of stanza 9, Spenser jars us with a discordant note, mentioning "the Maple seeldom inward sound." Fair on the outside, nature may be rotten within. This image, which becomes a kind of touchstone for Book One, implicitly comments on the attractive grove, looking forward to the monster that lurks inside and also glancing back at the opening picture of the knight fair outside but mysterious within.

The storm past, the couple realize they are lost. Judging the most beaten path the most promising, they discover that instead it leads to the heart of the labyrinth where they find an ominous hollow cave. The knight, a "champion stout," dismounts to investigate, but the lady warns him to beware:

> . . . Oft fire is without smoke,
> And perill without show: therefore your stroke
> Sir Knight with-hold, till further triall made.
> Ah Ladie (said he) shame were to revoke
> The forward footing for an hidden shade:
> Vertue gives her selfe light, through darkenesse for to
> wade. (i.12)

The lady speaks in maxims, and her warning in consequence sounds a bit fatuous so that we are not wholly out of sympathy with the knight's impatient response, even though his words about virtue giving light also have the pat sound of an adage. What Spenser is doing here—Shakespeare will do something similar when he has Polonius speak in maxims—is using the proverbial form of speech as symbolic of the inadequacy of his characters' conventional patterns of thought. But in fact only the knight's thought is conventional: the lady's maxim may sound familiar at first but, significantly, Spenser has had her reverse the usual proverb about smoke and fire.

The knight thinks of himself as the familiar hero of romance, bold, brave, and invincible because of his virtue. And it is of course precisely this conventional literary figure that Spenser evokes when he calls the man a "champion stout" and when, at the start of stanza 14, he uses a heroic phrase like "full of fire and greedy hardiment." But, immediately after employing this phrase, Spenser reminds us of the knight's youthfulness, and a moment later the pat adage about virtue giving light is at least somewhat qualified when the young man peers into the cave and Spenser tells us "his glistring armor made / A litle glooming light, much like a shade." In evoking and then qualifying a literary stereotype, the romance champion, Spenser is playing upon our responses as readers, beginning to educate us in the complexities of his world. In this literary world the conventional responses of a reader of romance are as naive and inadequate as the young man's aphorisms.

Although feeble, the knight's light allows him to see the monster clearly. Her name is Error—with a pun on *errare*, to wander, that associates her with the "wandring wood''—and the abstract name, introduced even before the knight peers into the cave, naturally influences the way we approach the figure. Error not only dwells in the heart of the forest but is the heart of the forest, the ugly and dangerous principle at its core. The knots and coils of her long tail recall the paths and alleys of the labyrinthine wood, and when, in the stuggle, she winds her tail about the knight to strangle him, we realize that the action is a sinister mirror of the earlier moment when the knight and lady became passively caught in the forest's maze. ''God helpe the man so wrapt in Errours endlesse traine,'' Spenser exclaims at the end of stanza 18, and the colloquial, almost worn-out, phrase ''God help'' is rejuvenated by the earnestness of its use.

Spenser's exclamation is immediately followed by help, though not by direct divine intervention:

> His Lady sad to see his sore constraint,
>   Cride out, Now now Sir knight, shew what ye bee,
>   Add faith unto your force, and be not faint:
>   Strangle her, else she sure will strangle thee.   (i.19)

Encouraged by this call to faith, the knight breaks the monster's hold. A call to faith, but faith in what? His lady? His own powers? God? The specific referent of ''faith'' is no more determinable than the specific meaning of ''error.'' Spenser's strategy here as elsewhere is to use generalized, abstract terms in very concrete dramatic situations. Because they are subject to many possible readings, the terms acquire a quasi-symbolic quality, and to limit their meaning prematurely would be as much a violation of the poem as to translate the image of the dark forest. What is important is not the precise meaning of the word but the general pattern suggested: sore beset, the knight is in need of faith.

Her hold loosed, the monster vomits, and here it is crucial that we first of all respond to the ugliness of the black flood of stinking "lumpes of flesh and gobbets raw" (i.20). But when a few lines later he tells us her "vomit full of bookes and papers was," Spenser requires us to respond intellectually rather than viscerally, recalling the knight and lady's error in misconstruing the storm and recognizing that Error is an intellectual monstrosity.

Stanza 21, a formal epic simile, compares the monstrous fertility of the dragon's "flood" with the overflowing Nile:

As when old father Nilus gins to swell
With timely pride above the Aegyptian vale,
His fattie waves do fertile slime outwell,
And overflow each plaine and lowly dale:
But when his later spring gins to avale,
Huge heapes of mudd he leaves, wherein there breed
Ten thousand kindes of creatures, partly male
And partly female of his fruitfull seed;
Such ugly monstrous shapes elswhere may no man reed.   (i.21)

Father Nile is both old and recurrently youthful, suggesting a kind of eternal natural principle that asserts itself repeatedly. But there are two distinct stages to the Nile's process, the earlier "timely pride" and the "later spring," which is the season responsible for the generation of the misshapen creatures. The less sinister "timely pride'' delicately recalls the forest trees ''yclad with sommers pride'' (i.7) and, like the trees, mirrors the knight's boldness, which is timely because of his youth, a season of life in which overconfidence in one's powers is natural. The ''later spring'' represents a further stage in ''overflowing,'' one in which monsters are produced, and this stage mirrors Error and her monstrous vomit. The simile thus suggests the difference between the knight and the dragon but also the connection between them: the knight is at an early stage in the process that leads to Error's monstrosity. Error herself, we recall from stanza 14, may once have been human in form, and she preserves some remnants of humanity, for, although her lower parts are serpentine, ''th'other halfe,'' Spenser says, ''did womans shape retaine.'' In battling Error, then, the knight is fighting for his life in a metaphorical as well as a literal sense: if he does not conquer Error he may become her.

In its sexuality the Nile simile harks back to the storm that originally drove the knight and lady into the forest. There the heavenly father made love to the earth by releasing a flood of rain into her lap. Here the sexuality is onanistic, without love or intercourse. Father Nile merely swells with pride—in Elizabethan usage ''pride'' has sexual connotations—and releases his seed to generate appropriately androgynous creatures, partly male and partly female. These are the kind of fruits that can be produced without a sexual partner by one who relies upon his own powers.

''Such ugly monstrous shapes elsewhere may no man reed,'' stanza 21 concludes, the emphatically placed

pun on "reed"—meaning both "see" and "read"—
carrying us back to the books and papers of Error's vomit. And this bookish motif is elaborated in the following
stanza when the monster's spawn of small, deformed
serpents is described as "fowle, and blacke as inke"
(i.22). They are, in effect, letters. As I suggested, we respond intellectually rather than emotionally to the
bookish motif, and as the motif is elaborated the images
become more and more comic. The effect is deflationary: the dragon and her spawn seem more grotesque
than frightening. This deflationary movement is for-
malized in stanza 23, a second epic simile, which compares the knight to a shepherd pestered by a cloud of
gnats.

But in stanza 24 the knight's position is again regard-
ed seriously, for, although Error's spawn may not be
able to hurt him, the dragon is still a threat:

> Thus ill bestedd, and fearefull more of shame,
>   Then of the certaine perill he stood in,
>   Halfe furious unto his foe he came,
>   Resolv'd in minde all suddenly to win,
>   Or soone to lose, before he once would lin.

"Fearefull more of shame" recalls the knight's earlier
protest against his lady's advice to be cautious: "shame
were to revoke / The forward footing for an hidden
shade." It is possible to read the first two lines of stanza
24 as simply an assertion of bravery: the young man
cares less for danger than for his reputation as a knight.
But by this time our ears should be sufficiently attuned
to Spenser's voice to hear a second, ironic, meaning.
Perhaps the young man, still overflowing with timely

pride, is so concerned with his conception of himself as an invincible knight that he does not fully understand the danger he is in. "Halfe furious" is a fine heroic phrase to describe his determination, but it can also mean "half mad." Naturally, neither reading cancels the other; the knight is heroic, but he is also young and limited to seeing things from a single, romantic point of view. Spenser's ambiguous language encourages us to see more complexly, to regard the knight from several perspectives at once.

Striking with "more then manly force" (i.24), the knight cuts off the dragon's head. But are we to take "more then manly force" literally, which would suggest that he has been helped by supernatural powers, or merely as a conventional epic hyperbole for the strength of his determination? Again, the ambiguity is unresolved: Spenser's point is more to raise the question than to provide a definite answer.

Once the source of their being is dead, the brood of little monsters soon destroys itself by feeding upon Error's blood—the action is a parody of the Christian sacrament—until their guts burst. In stanza 27 the lady ratifies the knight's victory, telling him he has proved his strength, and in stanza 28 the forest labyrinth, so confusing before, is easily escaped, Error being conquered.

The slaying of Error completes the first episode, which constitutes a kind of prologue to Book One, a foreshadowing in miniature—rather like the dumbshow introducing an early Elizabethan play—of the pattern to be worked out at large. We have only temporarily escaped from the dark forest: Spenser will return to explore its meanings more fully. Once again the knight and lady will wander. Once again the young man will need to add faith to his force and will discover that he has more than manly power. Moreover, all the motifs briefly evoked in the prologue—the knight's sad countenance, the trees of the forest, the flooding river, the dark cave, the monster with a woman's head—will return to be developed in increasingly subtle variations.

The opening episode serves as a prologue, but it is also an element in the sequential development of the story—the knight's first and simplest encounter with danger. We should notice that we are exactly midway in the first canto: the dragon episode has taken 27 stanzas; stanza 28, describing how the knight and lady find their way out of the forest and search for new adventure, forms a kind of pivot; and the canto's second episode, the adventure in Archimago's hermitage, occupies another 27 stanzas. Spenser's stanza, as I have already suggested, is one unit of structure. The canto is another. A Spenserian canto may be composed of a series of episodes, but it is always conceived as a coherent whole with the various episodes gaining in significance by being combined in a single large structure. The first canto may be thought of as a kind of diptych, with the two episodes balanced against each other like panels in a double painting placed side by side for comparison. The first panel shows the young knight's escape from an obvious danger; the second portrays his much more problematic adventure in the hermitage, where things are not so simply what they seem.

The second episode begins in much the same manner as the first, with a formal description of an anonymous character:

> At length they chaunst to meet upon the way
>   An aged Sire, in long blacke weedes yclad,
>   His feete all bare, his beard all hoarie gray,
>   And by his belt his booke he hanging had;
>   Sober he seemde, and very sagely sad,
>   And to the ground his eyes were lowly bent,
>   Simple in shew, and voide of malice bad,
>   And all the way he prayed, as he went,
> And often knockt his brest, as one that did repent.
>
> (i.29)

The knight is young, the hermit old—this contrast between youth and age is to become increasingly suggestive as the poem develops—but once again Spenser emphasizes that we are seeing only the man's exterior. This time, however, Spenser's language is so tentative, so cautionary, that our suspicions about what may lie beneath the holy surface are necessarily aroused. The travelers see only what the hermit wishes them to see, but we, who have learned to listen as well as see, hear the warning in Spenser's voice. Moreover, we can also hear a curious contradiction in what the hermit says: although he can control his appearance, from the first the man's words betray him. The knight inquires about adventures he might undertake, and the hermit informs him that there is a "daunger which hereby doth dwell," a "homebred evill" (i.31) in the form of an evil man laying waste to the countryside. But a moment later the hermit, perhaps playing to the young man's conventional sense of what a romantic adventure ought to be like, suggests that the danger is distant rather than near: "Far hence (quoth he) in wastfull wildernesse / His dwelling is, by which no living wight / May ever pass, but thorough great distresse" (i.32).

The confusion about the danger's location passes unnoticed as the lady, fearing her knight has no sense of his limits, advises him to rest before adventuring further, reminding him that even "The Sunne that measures heaven all day long, / At night doth baite his steedes the Ocean waves emong" (i.32). The old man quickly seconds her advice, suggesting that they take up their "In" at his hermitage. "So in they entred arre," the curt phrase with which the knight and lady wandered into the forest, is still ringing in our ears, and the old man's word sounds particularly ominous when we learn that his hermitage is situated "hard by a forests side." Nevertheless, Spenser concludes his description of the hermitage by calling to our attention that even here there is a gentle "Christall streame"—the spelling is significant—"Which from a sacred fountaine welled forth alway" (i.34).

Much of the special suggestiveness of *The Faerie Queene* depends upon insistent repetition of images and motifs, a technique through which Spenser develops an increasingly resonant pattern of allusion as the poem proceeds. Moreover, Spenser usually defines an event with multiple metaphors, each image reaching back to earlier images in the poem. Thus, entering the hermitage the knight is, in a sense, reentering the dark forest, but Spenser also defines the hermitage episode in terms of the lady's image of the sun sinking into the ocean. Like the heaven-traveling sun, the knight is about to descend into a watery element—we recall the overflowing Nile and also, by way of contrast, the rain of the opening storm—associated with darkness, oblivion, and sexuality. This image of decline has disturbing connotations, and yet the analogy with the sun suggests that perhaps the descent is natural, necessary, and temporary.

In stanza 36 Spenser describes the knight and lady falling asleep in language that develops the idea of immersion and makes us respond to the process from several points of view at once:

> The drouping Night thus creepeth on them fast,
>> And the sad humour loading their eye liddes,
>> As messenger of Morpheus on them cast
>> Sweet slombring deaw, the which to sleepe them
>>> biddes.
>> Unto their lodgings then his guestes he riddes:
>> Where when all drownd in deadly sleepe he findes,
>> He to his study goes, and there amiddes
>> His Magick bookes and artes of sundry kindes,
> He seekes out mighty charmes, to trouble sleepy
>> mindes.   (i.36)

That the night creeps, perhaps like a thief, evokes possibilities of deceit and dissimulation, and the generally inauspicious implications of this first line are reinforced by the second. ''Sad humour'' can mean ''dark vapor,'' but ''sad'' also picks up the suggestion of sorrowfulness in ''drouping.'' The third and fourth lines shift our perspective so that we respond more positively, the sad humor metamorphosing into ''sweet slombring deaw,'' which is what the knight and lady feel upon their eyes.

These four lines are wonderfully evocative of falling a-
sleep because the poetic technique itself imitates a semi-
somnolent state. The language dissolves the distinction
between outer and inner realities—''sad humour,'' for
instance, may refer to the mists of evening or alternatively to the body's own sleep-producing moisture—im-
mersing us in a fluid world of progressively modulating
emotions. Thus it comes as something of a jolt when in
line 5 we return to the world of concrete objects and see
the knight and lady with the hermit's cold objectivity,
''drownd in deadly sleepe.''

One of the first facts we learned about the hermit was
that he carried a book, and later we heard of his store of
''pleasing wordes'' (i.35). Naturally we assumed the
hermit's book to be a bible or breviary, but now the
ambiguity of that seemingly straightforward ''booke''
becomes apparent. Though a man of books and words,
the hermit is a conjurer rather than a priest. In stanza 27
Spenser describes his ''charmes'':

> Then choosing out few wordes most horrible,
> (Let none them read) thereof did verses frame,
> With which and other spelles like terrible,
> He bad awake blacke Plutoes griesly Dame,
> And cursed heaven, and spake reprochfull shame
> Of highest God, the Lord of life and light;
> A bold bad man, that dar'd to call by name
> Great Gorgon, Prince of darknesse and dead night,
> At which Cocytus quakes, and Styx is put to flight.
>
> (i.37)

The emphasis on books and words recalls Error's bookish
vomit, but in the first episode Spenser dwelt upon the
grotesqueness and impotence of evil words; now he

emphasizes the dreadful power of words that can awaken the dark forces of hell.

The hermit's name, as we discover after his nature has been revealed, is Archimago: the arch-magician or, even more appropriately, the arch-image-maker, a name that suggests the manner in which he creates a world of false images through spells, magical acts that parody God's original creation of the universe with the magic of the divine Word. Ultimately Spenser's poem is a battle of books, a contention, as we shall see, between Archimago's words and God's Word. Ultimately the contending forces that lie behind the story, like the contending forces in most romances, are two forms of magic, the diabolic and the divine. Spenser shows us Archimago speaking his spells, but the young knight is asleep and unconscious. I suggested earlier that one of the crucial things the knight must learn is the power of words: put somewhat differently, he must discover the supremacy of spirit over matter, must learn that the perceivable world is really the manifestation of spirit or, in the metaphor of Spenser's story, learn that there are enchanters at work in the world.

Describing the magician's spells, Spenser interjects a warning: "Let none them read." Playful in tone, Spenser is nonetheless deadly serious. If words are magical, the realization of the creating power of spirit, then to read Archimago's words would be to enter the diabolic world he creates. Putting it bluntly, Archimago's verses would enchant us. But Spenser does not let us read Archimago's spells: the verses we read are Spenser's own. Archimago, we should realize, is a kind of poet, Spenser's evil antithesis: all words are magical and all poets, in a sense, are magicians, arch-image-makers. The enchanting world of *The Faerie Queene* is no less magical than Archimago's creation, but the source of Spenser's power, as his invocations insist, is divine. If all worlds are ultimately spiritual, created by words, then the issue is not whether we can free ourselves from enchantment, but rather what kinds of spells we will listen to. The question for us as readers is the same as for the knight: will our image-makers be diabolic or divine?

With his spells Archimago conjures up legions of "sprights" which flutter around his head like "little flies." The image reflects the belief that evil spirits took the form of flies, but, more important, it echoes the earlier simile in which Error's spawn was compared to a cloud of gnats: dangerous as the magician is, his sprights are in themselves no more potent then Error's brood. Selecting two sprights, Archimago sends one down to the house of Morpheus, god of sleep, to procure a dream with which to plague the sleeping knight. The six stanzas that describe the spright's embassy, a kind of descent to hell, are comic in tone: certainly we should not miss the humor of the messenger's having to wake the god of sleep himself. The episode also permits Spenser to display his virtuosity, as in the onomatopoetic evocation of sleep in stanza 41. But the visit to Morpheus is more than a decorative digression from the main story. For one thing we should note that Morpheus' dark house, deep in the earth, is a cave, reminiscent of Error's den: once again the young knight will have to contend with a kind of monster emerging from a benighted cavern. Spenser's description of Morpheus' house goes beyond that of the earlier cave, however, fusing the earth imagery of the initial episode with the dominant water imagery of the present one. Morpheus' bed, washed continually by Tethys, wife of Ocean, is as moist as it is earthy. Morpheus himself is of course a personification of a psychic state, and the god "drowned deepe / In drowsie fit" (i.40) recalls the knight "drownd in deadly sleepe." Descending into this underworld of the lower elements, earth and water, we are in effect penetrating into the young knight's mind, being given a fully realized experience of his heedless, somnolent condition. In a sense the diabolic instrument, the false dream, that the spright procures from Morpheus is something brought forth from the dark depths of the knight's soul.

Spenser's narrative technique, especially his use of personification, often results in a radical ambiguity: again and again, as in the case of Morpheus, it is unclear whether a figure or event is external or internal, objective or psychic. This ambiguity is by no means a flaw, and we would be doing the poem a disservice if we attempted with lawyerlike logic to resolve it case by case. It would be equally limiting to maintain that everything in the poem is necessarily objective or, alternatively, to dissolve everything into a projection of some aspect of the protagonist. Instead we should recognize that the experience of the ambiguity is itself Spenser's "point." If the material world is magical, the creation of spirit, then there can be no clear distinction between the

external material world and the internal world of spirit,
for ultimately they are the same—which is precisely what
the poem in its ambiguity compels us to experience.

While one spright procures the dream, Archimago
fashions the other into a simulacrum of the knight's
lady, and, significantly, Spenser chooses the moment of
this second lady's creation for the first mention of the
name Una—the One. Before the false lady existed,
before duplicity in the sense both of doubleness and of
guile entered the poem, the lady had no need of a
name; now, however, her name itself stands in
opposition to the multiplicity of the world that
Archimago spawns.

Archimago sends the dream and the false lady to the
knight's chamber, making him "dreame of loves and
lustfull play, / That nigh his manly hart did melt away,
/ Bathed in wanton blis and wicked joy" (i.47). The
knight dreams that his lady offers herself to him, and
when he wakes the dream seems to have come true:

> In this great passion of unwonted lust,
>> Or wonted feare of doing ought amis,
>> He started up, as seeming to mistrust
>> Some secret ill, or hidden foe of his:
>> Lo there before his face his Lady is,
>> Under blake stole hiding her baited hooke,
>> And as halfe blushing offred him to kis,
>> With gentle blandishment and lovely looke,
> Most like that virgin true, which for her knight him
>> took.   (i.49)

The temptress created by Archimago is a delusion, a
distorted image of Una that is the projection of the
young man's own passion. Ironically, the knight has

awakened to another dream, more dangerous because apparently real. Spenser teases us with a hint that perhaps the knight will discover he has a "hidden foe," but, torn between sexual desire and fear of shaming himself, the young man is too confused to see the baited hook.

Controlling both his lust and his indignation, the knight wants to be sure he is not mistaken about the meaning of the lady's gestures or, as Spenser puts it, he "gan himselfe advise / To prove his sense, and tempt her faigned truth" (i.50). "To prove his sense" is the key to the episode, for the baited hook is not just the temptation to succumb to the lady's blandishments but the danger that, trusting the misleading evidence of his senses, the knight will believe that Archimago's spright is Una. The problem posed for the young man, in other words, is not so much a simple choice between lust and chastity, but a more important one between faith in the visible world and another kind of faith which in his youth and inexperience he cannot yet begin to understand.

The final note of the canto is positive. "Sliding softly forth" (i.54) in a disturbingly serpentine fashion, the lady departs, and the dream, after a last attempt to rouse the knight from lustful thoughts to action, admits defeat. The young man assumes that in not yielding to desire he has proved his virtue, as indeed he has. But whether he has been subverted in a more fundamental way is less certain.

Canto II

Spenser's cantos normally open with an image or general reflection designed to bring our experiences into focus before the poem moves on. The first stanza of canto II evokes a cosmic tableau that suggests a new and wider perspective on the nocturnal events in Archimago's hermitage:

> By this the Northerne wagoner had set
>> His sevenfold teme behind the stedfast starre,
>> That was in Ocean waves yet never wet,
>> But firme is fixt, and sendeth light from farre
>> To all, that in the wide deepe wandring arre:
>> And chearefull Chaunticlere with his note shrill
>> Had warned once, that Phoebus fiery carre
>> In hast was climbing up the Easterne hill,
> Full envious that night so long his roome did fill.
>
> (ii.1)

After the confusing watery world of dreams and apparitions, the simple, unambiguous image of the one firmly fixed star, the Pole Star that "was in Ocean waves yet never wet," comes as a relief and reassurance: Spenser reminds us that there is a heavenly beacon for sea wanderers—we recall the key term from the wandering wood episode. But even as the steadfast star comments upon the events of canto I, it also, as an emblem of constancy, is a primal image for canto II, which is concerned with faithlessness in love.

The issues at this point in Spenser's story are, we can

note, very similar to those in *Othello,* which is also concerned with a military man's loss of faith in his lady. Deceived by Iago, as the young knight is by Archimago, Othello loses his way by naively trusting the evidence of his senses, the ''ocular proof'' of Desdemona's unworthiness. Like Iago, Archimago works upon his victim in careful stages. Canto I ended with the young knight in confusion, his doubts roused but not confirmed. Now, at the start of canto II, Archimago employs his sprights to provide ocular proof of Una's unworthiness, arranging a spectacle in which the knight sees what he supposes to be his lady making love with a squire: ''Which when he saw, he burnt with gealous fire, / The eye of reason was with rage yblent'' (ii.5). Ironically, the effect of trusting his vision is a form of blindness.

Tormented by his ''guiltie sight''—the phrase is a double entendre—the knight returns to bed until dawn: ''Then up he rose, and clad him hastily; / The Dwarfe him brought his steed: so both away do fly'' (ii.6). ''So both away do fly''—with this phrase, marking his separation from Una, the knight's wanderings begin in earnest, and we should remark that in placement, tone, and rhythm the phrase recalls that earlier half-line of initiation at the start of canto I: ''so in they entred arre.'' The knight imagines he is fleeing a labyrinth of confusion and faithlessness, but in fact, as the echo of the earlier phrase suggests, he is entering another.

After the young man's hasty departure in stanza 6, Spenser's tone changes, becoming sweetly lyrical as he describes a contrasting arising from bed:

Now when the rosy-fingred Morning faire,
    Weary of aged Tithones saffron bed,
    Had spred her purple robe through deawy aire,
    And the high hils Titan discovered,
    The royall virgin shooke off drowsy-hed,
    And rising forth out of her baser bowre,
    Lookt for her knight, who far away was fled,
    And for her Dwarfe, that wont to wait each houre;
Then gan she waile and weepe, to see that woefull
    stowre.   (ii.7)

The lyrical image of the dawn leaving her lover's bed affects our emotional response to Una, as lovely as the morning, and enhances the pathos of her abandonment. Moreover, in its evocation of a relationship between an old man and an eternally youthful goddess—Aurora seems to be weary of Tithonus' bed because he is aged—the image comments wittily on Una's night in the old man's hermitage, applying a classical fable to a situation in which age and youth have Christian symbolic overtones. The general image of love between a divinity and a man is also, of course, suggestive.

Una sets out in pursuit of her knight, but his "light-foot steede"—the familiar classical epithet acquires an ironic meaning—spurred by "wrath and fiery fierce disdaine" (ii.8), has already carried him so far that catching up is impossible. Spenser's reference to the horse recalls its initial appearance in canto I, angrily foaming at the bit. Then the knight was having difficulty controlling his mount; now he has loosed the reins and the danger implicit in that original image of barely restrained energy has begun to be realized.

Ironically, the very quality that makes the young man a hero, his spiritedness, is now betraying him, propelling him away from his love.

Stanzas 9, 10, and 11 shift our attention to Archimago, rejoicing at having divided his guests into "double parts." As I suggested earlier, Book One—the book's number is symbolic—is concerned with unity versus multiplicity, with the singleness of the divine versus diabolic duplicity. Archimago is the very principle of multiplicity, and Spenser emphasizes this in stanza 10, telling us how the magician possesses Proteus' power to change his shape at will, appearing by turns a fowl, a fish, a fox, and a dragon, this last form being so terrible "That of himselfe he oft for feare would quake, / And oft would flye away." The four creatures illustrating Archimago's power, each associated with one of the ancient "elements," air, water, earth, and fire, suggest his domination over the entire material world. That he can appear as a dragon obviously associates him with Error, and we should not miss the humor and significance of Archimago's being the victim of his own power, taking on forms so dreadful that he tries to fly from himself in fear. At the moment, however, the form he takes on is that of the young knight, and Spenser repeats word for word, but with very different force in the verb "seemde," one of the phrases from the initial description of the young man: "Full jolly knight he seemde." It is here, too, that Spenser reveals the young knight's name, Saint George. Just as Una's name was irrelevant before the false Una was created, so the knight's name is first used when

Archimago takes on his appearance. In the original oneness, before evil enters the world, virtue needs no name; now that we have begun to discover evil we can also begin to understand who the young man is. The thought is not unlike Milton's in *Areopagitica*: "It was from out the rind of one apple tasted, that the knowledge of good and evil, as two twins cleaving together, leaped forth into the world. And perhaps this is the doom which Adam fell into of knowing good and evil, that is to say of knowing good by evil."

The first eleven stanzas, describing the knight's departure from his lady, his inconstancy, and concluding with Archimago's shape changing, his metamorphoses, constitute the prologue to canto II, an initial statement of theme. The body of the canto consists of two significantly paired episodes, the knight's conquest of Sansfoy's lady and his encounter with Fradubio, which develop the implications of the theme.

The link between the prologue and the first major episode, the shift from Archimago to the knight, is made in terms of the knight's name. We have just heard at the end of stanza 11 that Archimago in disguise looks so much like the young knight that we might suppose him to be Saint George. Stanza 12 begins: "But he the knight, whose semblaunt he did beare, / The true Saint George was wandred far away, / Still flying from his thoughts and gealous fear." The knight himself, so much more naive about his world than we are, does not know his name, and this is the last time until canto X, when he discovers his identity, that Spenser uses it; until then he will refer to him simply as the Knight of the Redcross. More important, the reference to Redcross flying from his thoughts, from himself, mirrors Archimago's self-deception, his frightened flying from his own dragonish shape. The young knight and Archimago now look uncomfortably similar. Yet appearances, we know, are not to be trusted: we as readers are being asked to keep faith in the young man's virtue despite ocular proof to the contrary.

The need to look beyond appearances is again Spenser's point in the Sansfoy episode, where he plays upon our response to allegory as a literary mode. The first explicitly allegorical figure that Redcross encountered was Error; now he meets another, Sansfoy or Faithlessness, whose name is emblazoned on his shield:

> At last him chaunst to meete upon the way
> A faithlesse Sarazin all arm'd to point,
> In whose great shield was writ with letters gay
> Sans foy: full large of limbe and every joint
> He was, and cared not for God or man a point. (ii.12)

In the episode that follows, Redcross slays Sansfoy—as is commonly the case in allegories, their enmity is unmotivated: the Christian and Saracen simply represent antagonistic principles—and becomes the new champion of the pagan's lady, Fidessa. The name Sansfoy prepares us to read the battle allegorically and indeed the meaning is transparent: the Christian hero conquers Faithlessness and frees the Faithful, represented by the distressed lady, from bondage.

In fact the meaning is too transparent. (In its simplicity it perhaps reminds us of the hermit's ostentatious simplicity in canto I.) Redcross naturally regards himself as the heroic embodiment of faith triumphing over faithlessness, but how can we, knowing that in abandoning Una he has just proved himself a man of little faith, accept this allegory at face value? Indeed, Spenser has organized the episode so that we are encouraged to look beyond its appearance of simplicity. We should note, for example, that the simple opposition of Christian and Saracen is qualified by the way Spenser's language suggests similarities between the knights. In stanza 15 Redcross and Sansfoy are equally ''fell and furious'' as they charge each other, and then in stanza 16 Spenser gives us an extended simile comparing the knights to battling rams:

> As when two rams stird with ambitious pride,
>> Fight for the rule of the rich fleeced flocke,
>> Their horned fronts so fierce on either side
>> Do meete, that with the terrour of the shocke
>> Astonied both, stand sencelesse as a blocke,
>> Forgetfull of the hanging victory:
>> So stood these twaine, unmoved as a rocke,
>> Both staring fierce, and holding idely
> The broken reliques of their former cruelty.

This simile is related to the face value of the allegory: the image of a struggle over a flock draws upon traditional Christian pastoral motifs, suggesting a contention for rule of the faithful. But the usual master of the flock in Christian pastoral is the shepherd; here the contenders are rams ''stird with ambitious pride.'' ''Pride,'' as I mentioned earlier, often has sexual as well as heroic and moral overtones; and so does ''horned,'' an appropriate word since Redcross believes his lady has betrayed him. What the simile's sexual allusions suggest is hardly a struggle between good and evil but rather a contest for domination between two aroused animals. Moreover, the simile emphasizes both contenders' obliviousness, the way they stand "astonied," forgetful of what they are fighting for, implying that Redcross no less than the unenlightened Saracen is ignorant both of his own motives and of the real issues in contention.

The irony becomes more intense as the episode proceeds. After his victory, Redcross takes possession of the Saracen's shield as his rightful prize. But the shield is labeled "Faithlessness," and now he is its bearer. Now, too, he becomes the champion of the pagan's companion, whom Spenser has treated with heavy irony from the beginning:

> He had a faire companion of his way,
>   A goodly Lady clad in scarlot red,
>   Purfled with gold and pearle of rich assay,
>   And like a Persian mitre on her hed
>   She wore, with crownes and owches garnished,
>   The which her lavish lovers to her gave;
>   Her wanton palfrey all was overspred
>   With tinsell trappings, woven like a wave,
> Whose bridle rung with golden bels and bosses brave.
> (ii.13)

Details in this description associate the lady both with the Whore of Babylon from the Book of Revelations and with the Roman Catholic Church, but, having already met Una, we do not need biblical or historical knowledge to respond negatively to the lady's attire, which contrasts completely with Una's modest white gown and black stole: whatever else she may be, this new lady is evidently not straightforward and simple. Her "wanton palfrey" also obviously contrasts with Una's humble ass, and the palfrey's trappings, "woven like a wave," recall the water imagery of the hermitage episode, suggesting that here is another kind of ocean in which a sea wanderer might drown.

After Sansfoy's death the lady presents herself as a damsel in distress, and Redcross readily accepts Fidessa's name and story, which perfectly fit his conception of himself as the champion of faith. Redcross is also vulnerable for another reason. As the simile of the rams implied, his motives in the fight with Sansfoy were more complex than he realized. Unfamiliar forces have been at work in him since his night in the hermitage and Spenser reminds us of this now, revealing that he has been in "great passion" during the lady's speech, "More busying his quicke eyes, her face to view, / Then his dull eares, to heare what she did tell" (ii.26). Words still mean little to Redcross, but we, whose ears are not dull, can hear the fatuity in the maxim with which in the next stanza he pledges himself to be the lady's defender: "Better new friend then an old foe is said" (ii.27). And with playful irony Spenser concludes the stanza and the episode by burlesquing the young man's penchant for aphorisms: "So forth they rode, he feining seemely merth, / And she coy lookes: so dainty they say maketh derth."

Stanzas 28 and 29 provide the transition between the Sansfoy and Fradubio episodes, describing how Redcross and his new lady, hot and weary, rest themselves in a little oasis of shade made of two trees, "their greene leaves trembling with every blast" (ii.28). The leaves' trembling suggests fearfulness and uncertainty, recalling by way of contrast the firmness of the opening stanza's "stedfast starre." Moreover, there is something ominous about the trees and their shadow, for shepherds, we are told, shun the spot.

> But this good knight soone as he them can spye,
>   For the coole shade him thither hastly got:
>   For golden Phoebus now ymounted hie,
>   From fiery wheeles of his faire chariot
>   Hurled his beame so scorching cruell hot,
>   That living creature mote it not abide;
>   And his new Lady it endured not.
>   There they alight, in hope themselves to hide
> From the fierce heat, and rest their weary limbs a tide.
>   (ii.29)

The situation echoes the earlier entry into the wandering wood. Once again Redcross seeks to escape the effects of a sky god's activity, this time Phoebus, the sun. He thinks only of hiding from the scorching heat but the sun's heat is inextricably associated with its light, and in withdrawing into the coolness of the shade he is also retreating into darkness.

At Archimago's hermitage Una advised Redcross to sleep, remarking that even the strongest man "wanting rest will also want of might" (i.32). Unable to sleep soundly then, the knight is unable to bear the heat of the day now. At least for the moment he is abandoning his "traveil": Spenser employs this word as a pun throughout Book One. Having withdrawn from heroic activity, from the forward motion of a quest that has become confused and problematic since he has lost faith in Una, it is appropriate that he encounters, as a kind of warning, an image of complete immobility—Fradubio, a man transformed into a tree. Fradubio's name, Brother Doubt, points both to his crucial error, lack of faith, and to his relationship with Redcross. But Redcross, having withdrawn from the light, never perceives that this bizarre creature is his alter ego, the image of what he himself is in danger of becoming.

The episode, which has antecedents in Vergil, Dante, and Ariosto, begins as Redcross plucks a bough to make a garland for his new lady; the tree cries out in pain, warning him to flee "Least to you hap, that happened to me heare" (ii.31). It is appropriate that the cry interrupts Redcross' garland making, for in a sense the burden of the episode is a warning not to crown Fidessa as his mistress. The knight is understandably terrified to hear a tree speak, and yet we should not miss the irony of the fact that in his fear he becomes as rigid as the tree itself: "Astond he stood, and up his haire did hove, / And with that suddein horror could no member move" (ii.31). His terror past and assured that the creature is neither a ghost nor a spirit, Redcross rather condescendingly asks Fradubio how he became so "misshaped," and the tree replies with a story of inconstancy in love that is the mirror of the knight's own history.

Having defeated a stranger knight and won his lady—we recall Redcross' pyrrhic victory over Sansfoy—Fradubio found himself uncertain who was more worthy of being crowned with the garland of love, his own mistress, Fraelissa, or the new lady. What Fradubio did not know as he stood suspended in doubt—in a Dantesque manner, his present physical immobility is the image of his former indecision—was that the new lady was a witch, Duessa. Just as Archimago deceived Redcross into believing Una unworthy, so Duessa breathed a magical fog into Fraelissa's face, dimming her beauty. Fradubio, vulnerable to magic because of his lack of faith in Fraelissa, changed his allegiance and abandoned his former mistress. Later he discovered Duessa bathing and, seeing her ugliness, realized his mistake. The image of Duessa in the water, her "neather partes misshapen, monstruous" (ii.41), recalls Error, the monster with a woman's face and distorted, serpentine nether parts. But even though he perceived his error, Fradubio, lacking faith to add to his force, was powerless before the witch. Realizing that he planned to flee, Duessa transformed him into a tree and planted him next to his old love, Fraelissa, and together they must stand until released by being "bathed in a living well" (ii.43).

The mysterious promise of the "living well," magical waters that suggest baptism, is reassuring. But the image of a living man transformed into a tree is not. The Fradubio episode suggests that Redcross is in danger of being transformed, at least metaphorically, into something less than human. The young man naturally assumes that his own shape is constant and that Fradubio is merely a pitiable monster, not, in a sense, his brother. But then he also assumes that he has been the model of constancy in love. Redcross' ignorance is rooted in his trust in nature, his belief in physical rather than spiritual or magical reality. In the world of this poem, a world in which trees turn out to be enchanted men, nature itself, we are beginning to realize, is "seeldom inward sound." But Redcross, believing still in the evidence of his senses, is trapped in nature, intellectually imprisoned, just as his brother in faithlessness is physically imprisoned.

We have long been suspicious of Redcross' new lady, and during Fradubio's speech our suspicions have increased. Now, at the end of the canto, Spenser confirms our expectations, revealing that "Fidessa" is the same Duessa who enchanted Fradubio. In canto II—possibly the number is significant—Redcross has abandoned Una, the One, and joined Duessa, becoming lost in doubleness, in the forest of the world of appearance. Yet even as at the start of the episode he sought the cool shade, so at the end he seems to be willfully avoiding recognition:

> . . . But the good knight
> Full of sad feare and ghastly dreriment,
> When all this speech the living tree had spent,
> The bleeding bough did thrust into the ground,
> That from the bloud he might be innocent,
> And with fresh clay did close the wooden wound:
> Then turning to his Lady, dead with feare her found.
>
> (ii.44)

The young man fears implication in Fradubio's history: the "living tree" has spent its speech in vain. In turning to Duessa, "dead with feare," Redcross has in effect turned his back upon life.

But, although Duessa may in one sense be death

itself, the witch is only feigning fright, and in the final stanza she readily allows her knight to revive her:

> . . . with trembling cheare
> Her up he tooke, too simple and too trew,
> And oft her kist. At length all passed feare,
> He set her on her steede, and forward forth did beare.
>
> (ii.45)

"Too simple and too trew"—this is the way the young man regards Duessa, but the line's grammatical ambiguity is calculated so that we can apply the phrase to Redcross as well. The knight's "trembling cheare" ominously recalls the tree's trembling leaves, and yet, like the first canto, the second apparently concludes affirmatively as Redcross overcomes his fear and immobility and moves forward again. But is the final note really positive? Redcross is moving, but in what direction?

Canto III

In basic narrative outline Spenser's poem, so complex in its details, is remarkably simple, the story of two lovers separated, wandering, and finally reunited. The middle part of the narrative follows each lover's adventures by turn: canto II dealt with Redcross; canto III shifts our attention to Una, the unjustly abandoned lady.

With the shift to Una, the poem changes mode. The appeal of canto II, ironic throughout, was primarily to our understanding: Spenser required that we interpret the young man's adventures, seeing through appearances so that we would not make the same intellectual errors as Redcross. At the start of canto III the irony largely disappears and the appeal is primarily to our emotions. The opening stanzas, in which Spenser directs our response to Una by describing his own, establish the new note.

> Nought is there under heav'ns wide hollownesse,
>   That moves more deare compassion of mind,
>   Then beautie brought t'unworthy wretchednesse
>   Through envies snares or fortunes freakes unkind:
>   I, whether lately through her brightnesse blind,
>   Or through alleageance and fast fealtie,
>   Which I do owe unto all woman kind,
>   Feele my heart perst with so great agonie,
> When such I see, that all for pittie I could die.
>
> And now it is empassioned so deepe,
>   For fairest Unaes sake, of whom I sing,

> That my fraile eyes these lines with teares do steepe,
> To thinke how she through guilefull handeling,
> Though true as touch, though daughter of a king,
> Though faire as ever living wight was faire,
> Though nor in word nor deede ill meriting,
> Is from her knight divorced in despaire
> And her due loves deriv'd to that vile witches share.
>
> (iii. 1-2)

This pathetic mood will remain dominant throughout the canto as we follow Una's unhappy wanderings. We may miss the ironic complexity of the earlier parts of the poem, but it would be a mistake to dismiss the pathos as sentimental. For one thing, the poet's self-consciousness is evident: Spenser hardly expects us to suppose that he is so caught up in his character's troubles that he literally writes with tears in his eyes. The emotionalism is ostentatious rather than in any modern sense "sincere" but it is by no means self-indulgent, for it is designed, like everything else in the poem, with didactic purpose. In the letter to Raleigh that he printed in the first edition of *The Faerie Queene,* Spenser explained that his "generall end" was "to fashion a gentleman or noble person in vertuous and gentle discipline." But fashioning readers in virtuous discipline does not, for Spenser at any rate, mean exhorting us in the manner of a preacher to live well; rather his poem is designed to educate our intellects and our emotions by making us think and feel effectively. Accomplish this, Spenser might say, and acting well will inevitably follow. In canto II Spenser was teaching us to think, to judge; now he is teaching us to feel, reminding us of the complementary principle of compassion, the human equivalent of the divine mercy manifested through grace. Canto II ended with the promise of a "living well": the phrase perhaps has a plain sense, living well as opposed to living poorly, in addition to the theological sense of regeneration through baptism. Now Spenser begins to suggest the nature of these merciful waters, associated like the erotic seas with love, but love of a much less selfish kind.

The action begins as Una, weary after long searching for her knight, retreats into "secret shadow" and removes her outer garments. Her "angels face," as Spenser describes it, shines out in the darkness like the sun: "Did never mortall eye behold such heavenly grace" (iii.4). Una's withdrawal recalls Redcross' weary retreat in canto II, but the contrast in the way we are asked to respond is striking. As I suggested earlier, much of Spenser's density derives from his insistent repetition of images and formulaic actions. Yet a formulaic action can bear many different meanings, and here the emphasis falls not so much on Una's retreat from sunlight as on the sun she has within her, her inward soundness in the form of "heavenly grace," a phrase that implies precisely what Redcross in his own shadowy place requires. The image of Una as a light in the midst of darkness is also an emblem that looks forward to the entire action of canto III.

As Una rests, a ferocious lion suddenly rushes from the "thickest wood." By now all forests have general associations with nature as well as specific echoes of the wandering wood, and that this lion comes from the woods' thickest part, nature's very heart, is especially disconcerting. But Spenser is manipulating us to surprise us, for instead of devouring Una the lion falls at her feet overcome by her beauty, and Una herself, amazed at the creature's gentleness, melts with compassion and sheds "drizling teares" that remind us of the poet's compassionate tears at the beginning. It is ironic that a mere beast should be kind when Redcross was cruel, and Una laments her lord's unkindness in a formal complaint which the forest—that is, nature itself—softly echoes. Earlier Spenser emphasized the dangers of trusting nature; now, when we have learned to be wary, he emphasizes the more positive side, stressing the degree to which benevolence is natural and the natural world is well-meaning.

With the lion as her "faithfull mate"—the phrase suggests both the beast's role as a surrogate Redcross and its ultimate inadequacy as a permanent companion for a lady—Una continues her wandering through the "deserts wide." The next episode, Una's night in Corceca's house, requires a certain amount of historical knowledge to be fully comprehensible, for Spenser is alluding to Henry VIII's suppression of the monasteries. Briefly, Corceca—Blind Heart—is the mother of Abessa who, as her name suggests, represents the monastic orders. Abessa has a lover, Kirkrapine, who despoils churches, bestowing their riches upon this daughter of ignorance and superstition. Kirkrapine visits Abessa nightly, but this evening when he arrives the lion, who for the moment suggests King Henry, seizes and dismembers him. Spenser tells us that "the thirstie land / Drunke up his life" (iii.20), which perhaps alludes to the sale of the monastic estates.

Some knowledge of Tudor history is helpful, but Spenser has not suddenly digressed from the main line of his story, and it is possible to read the episode in a purely narrative context. From the start of the canto, Una has been wandering in a barren, unpeopled landscape that is plainly no place for a lady. She has acquired the lion as a defender, and the beast's concern is touching but reminds us, nevertheless, how much she requires refuge in a human context. In introducing the Corceca episode, Spenser holds out the possibility of just such a civilized refuge. Una traveled, he tells us, through a country without a sign of "living wight," until "at length she found the troden gras, / In which the tract of peoples footing was" (iii.10). Following this promising path, she discovers a maiden carrying a water-pot on her "shoulders sad." But when she asks the girl if there is a dwelling nearby, Abessa is unable to reply: "She could not heare, nor speake, nor understand" (iii.11). Abessa runs home in fear to her blind mother, who spends day and night in constant prayer, and there Una finds the two of them, cowering in a dark corner. The lady requests a night's lodging, receives no answer, and simply lies down in weary necessity. What Spenser emphasizes, then, is the sadness, the pathetic inadequacy of this fearful mother and daughter as representatives of humanity; compared to them, the lion is a superior creature.

At dawn Una continues her search for Redcross, and Spenser compares her pains to Odysseus', "that long wandring Greeke, / That for his love refused deitie" (iii.21). Rather than living like a god with Calypso,

Odysseus chose the arduous labor of returning to his wife, Penelope. The simile adds a heroic note to the pathos of Una's situation, reminding us that she is not merely an abandoned lady, that her labors are also the result of her love for Redcross. Moreover, it comments retroactively on Corceca, who prays constantly—is Spenser suggesting that, in an ironic sense, she has withdrawn into "deitie"?—and in her fear and selfishness is incapable of compassion for the distressed. Too great boldness may be folly, but fear like Corceca's is for Spenser even more dangerous. We recall Fradubio's trembling leaves: in Spenser's world one must be a hero or lapse into something less than fully human.

This pattern of promise and disillusionment is repeated in the next episode, Una's encounter with Archimago disguised as Redcross. Again the lady believes she has found human refuge—the best refuge of all, her own knight—and again her hopes are dashed. This episode parallels the false Una's deception of Redcross, but whereas he was vulnerable because of his lack of faith, Una is vulnerable because of her desire to believe in her knight's worthiness: her weakness is her love. As before, the reader knows more than the character—Spenser tells us immediately that the knight is Archimago—but here the effect of the dramatic irony is pathos rather than satire.

Spenser manipulates our response especially subtly in this episode. We should note, for instance, in stanza 30 the way he delicately undercuts Una's joy, her readiness to accept the knight's explanation for his disappearance, by employing an aphorism, telling us that the knight's loving words seemed to her sufficient recompense for all her unhappiness: ''A dram of sweet is worth a pound of sowre.'' Given the way aphorisms have been used earlier in the poem, this necessarily sounds rather hollow. The stanza continues with another pathetically appropriate conventional thought: ''true love hath no powre / To looken backe; his eyes be fixt before. / Before her stands her knight, for whom she toild so sore.''

This ironic last line leads into the extended simile of stanza 31, in which Spenser gathers all the poem's water imagery, reaching back even to the pun on ''arbor'' and ''harbor'' when the knight and lady first entered the wandering wood:

> Much like, as when the beaten marinere,
>   That long hath wandred in the Ocean wide,
>   Oft soust in swelling Tethys saltish teare,
>   And long time having tand his tawney hide
>   With blustring breath of heaven, that none
>   can bide,
>   And scorching flames of fierce Orions hound,
>   Soone as the port from farre he has espide,
>   His chearefull whistle merrily doth sound,
> And Nereus crownes with cups; his mates
>   him pledg around.

Spenser leads us to assume that it is the knight who is being compared to the ''beaten marinere.'' And indeed the simile itself reinforces this assumption by the way it seems to recapitulate Redcross' watery wandering and his weariness of the heat. Yet we know that the simile cannot really apply to the knight, who is not Redcross but Archimago, and at the start of stanza 32 we learn that it is Una's emotion that is being described: "Such joy made Una, when her knight she found." Employing a marvelous grammatical ambiguity, Spenser has evoked a sense of what it would be like if Redcross had come at last to "port," thus intensifying the pathos when he reminds us that the joy is Una's alone and that she is deceived. What the knight—that is, Archimago—in fact feels is quite a different kind of pleasure, suggested in a comparison that is a parody of the "beaten marinere" simile. Finding Una thoroughly deceived, Archimago is as happy as a "glad marchant, that does vew from ground / His ship farre come from watrie wildernesse" (iii.32). Una for him is a venture, a business proposition, and of course he has not been to sea at all.

Archimago, the seeming knight who is inward unsound, is another surrogate Redcross, and his inadequacy as Una's defender is proved by his failure in the encounter with Sansloy. We first heard of this pagan knight in canto II after Redcross defeated Sansfoy, when Fidessa explained that Sansfoy was the eldest of three brothers, "bloudy bold" Sansloy being the second and Sansjoy the youngest. The order of birth suggests a causal sequence: faithlessness comes first, then lawlessness or chaos, then joylessness, and this is the order in which we meet the brothers in the story. Spying the Christian armor, Sansloy attacks and easily overthrows Una's companion. But when he removes the fallen knight's helmet, he discovers not the enemy he expected but a friend. Redcross' victory over Sansfoy was, we remember, more problematic than it seemed, for he inherited the pagan's shield and lady, becoming in effect the defender of faithlessness. Ironically, in his present condition Redcross is actually the friend of lawlessness, and it is appropriate that this encounter between his image and Sansloy should conclude with Sansloy ultimately saluting the false Christian champion as his friend. Moreover, given Redcross' general lack of awareness, it is also appropriate that his surrogate, lying unconscious on the ground, does not understand Sansloy's greeting: "He answered nought, but in a traunce still lay, / And on those guilefull dazed eyes of his / The cloud of death did sit" (iii.39).

The lion is the key to the structure of this canto. Introduced at the beginning, the beast proved nobler than the human beings at Corceca's house, and now he proves nobler than the cowardly false knight, for, seeing Una in Sansloy's hands, he attacks the pagan. The lion has strength but so does Sansloy, and the pagan has human intelligence besides: he "feates of armes did wisely understand" (iii.42). It is an unequal battle and the lion is quickly slain. Brave though he is, this representative of nature's nobility cannot protect Una. The beast's inadequacy was implicit from the beginning, and now at the canto's end it is confirmed.

Canto III concludes as it opened, with extreme pathos as Una, piteously lamenting, is carried off by Sansloy. Spenser rhetorically asks who is left to defend the forlorn maid. The final image is of another faithful beast, Una's mount, following "To be partaker of her wandring woe," and the last line, referring to the mount and pointing the contrast between animal and man, summarizes the theme of the canto as a whole: "More mild in beastly kind, then that her beastly foe" (iii.44).

Canto IV

Canto IV returns to Redcross, the first stanza providing a transition from the emotionalism of canto III to
a sterner mood as Spenser expounds the importance of
fidelity and passes judgment on his aspiring hero: "For
unto knight there is no greater shame, / Then lightnesse
and inconstancie in love; / That doth this Redcrosse
knights ensample plainly prove." The action proper
begins in stanza 2 when Redcross and Duessa see an
imposing palace in the distance and leading to it a broad
highway reminiscent of the beaten path that led to
Error.

The contrast between forest and court, country and
city, is central in the metaphorical structure of Spenser's
poem. Canto III has shown Una wandering in woods and
wildernesses, unsuccessfully seeking civilization and a
human protector, and since leaving the hermitage
Redcross, too, has been wandering in deserted lands and
frightening groves. In a sense all of Book One is a search
for the way out of the forest, the Wood of Error. Put
more positively, Spenser's fable is the search for a city, a
community in which men can live fully as men rather
than struggling for survival in the loneliness of the
wilderness.

Much of the effect of canto IV, the complexity
of our response to Lucifera's House of Pride,
depends upon our experience of the misery of the
wilderness in canto III. In order to appreciate the

fullness of Spenser's vision, we need to understand that
the purposes of those who flock to the House of Pride
are not altogether despicable, and of course the
aspiration of Lucifera, mistress of the house, is similar to
Redcross' own desire for glory. Nevertheless, Spenser
warns us of danger here. Many enter but few return,
and those disgraced and beggared escapees can be seen
lying like "loathsome lazars" by the hedges:
"Thither," Spenser says with chilling directness,
"Duessa bad him bend his pace" (iv.3). The House of
Pride represents Duessa's solution to the human problem, and the point of the episode is the total inadequacy of that way of life to satisfy authentic human
needs.

The description in stanzas 4 and 5 emphasizes the
palace's corporeality, for one of the fundamental
inadequacies of the House of Pride is that it represents a
material solution to spiritual needs.

> A stately Pallace built of squared bricke,
>   Which cunningly was without morter laid,
>   Whose wals were high, but nothing strong,
>   nor thick,
>   And golden foile all over them displaid,
>   That purest skye with brightnesse they dismaid:
>   High lifted up were many loftie towres,
>   And goodly galleries farre over laid,
>   Full of faire windowes, and delightfull bowres;
> And on the top a Diall told the timely howres.
>
> It was a goodly heape for to behould,
>   And spake the praises of the workmans wit;
>   But full great pittie, that so faire a mould
>   Did on so weake foundation ever sit:

For on a sandie hill, that still did flit,
And fall away, it mounted was full hie,
That every breath of heaven shaked it:
And all the hinder parts, that few could spye,
Were ruinous and old, but painted cunningly.

The architects have disguised the House of Pride's weaknesses, but, wholly of the earth, a structure of this kind can never last: the surmounting "Diall" implies its subjection to time, and the foundation of sand steadily falling away—the image evokes an hourglass—suggests that it is built upon impermanence. Spenser's irony is obvious, and many of the suggestive details, for example, the way the lofty house is shaken by heaven's breath, require no comment. But we should notice the subtle echo of Duessa's and Error's ugly nether regions in the final image of ruinous "hinder parts." Goodly in appearance, the castle is, nevertheless, inwardly unsound.

Redcross and Duessa enter and, passing through a crowded hall, reach the "maiden Queene"—she is for Spenser the parodic antithesis of his own maiden Queen Elizabeth—whose glory overwhelms their "fraile amazed senses." The lady's appeal is to the senses, faculties that are, as we learned in the hermitage episode, frail and not to be trusted. Once again, as in the formal portrait of the palace, what we see, the visual splendor that Spenser evokes, is belied by what we hear, the verbal appeal to our understanding:

High above all a cloth of State was spred,
And a rich throne, as bright as sunny day,
On which there sate most brave embellished
With royall robes and gorgeous array,

A maiden Queene, that shone as Titans ray,
  In glistring gold, and peerelesse pretious stone:
  Yet her bright blazing beautie did assay
  To dim the brightnesse of her glorious throne,
As envying her selfe, that too exceeding shone.

Exceeding shone, like Phoebus fairest childe,
  That did presume his fathers firie waine,
  And flaming mouthes of steedes unwonted wilde
  Through highest heaven with weaker hand to
    raine;
  Proud of such glory and advancement vaine,
  While flashing beames do daze his feeble eyen,
  He leaves the welkin way most beaten plaine,
  And rapt with whirling wheeles, inflames the
    skyen,
With fire not made to burne, but fairly for to shine.
                                             (iv.8-9)

The initial impression is of a blaze of light, an earthly
sun, an image that recalls Una's radiance in canto III.
There Spenser simply told us that Una's beauty "made
a sunshine in the shadie place" (iii.4); here the rhetoric
is more strident, producing a sense of strain that
reinforces the description of the competition between
the lady and her throne. We should notice that in the
last lines of stanza 8 Spenser shifts from an objective to a
subjective point of view, suggesting the insecurity
beneath the queen's display of magnificence. The lady,
who evidently imagines competitors everywhere, regards
even her throne as envious of her beauty, criticizing her
for shining with excessive brilliance. Her jealousy of an
inanimate object implies how totally she is immersed in

the material world. ''Exceeding shone''—with fine point Spenser repeats the words at the start of stanza 9 as he comments on her shining, comparing her to Phaethon, who fell in flames when he presumed to drive Apollo's sun chariot but could not manage his father's steeds. The simile, which hints at Satan's fall from heaven, implies that the lady is usurping a god's place. Moreover, the image of the steeds running wild recalls Redcross' difficulty in controlling his horse: this lady has in effect entirely loosed the reins of her ambitious spirit, and the result, Spenser suggests, is bound to be disastrous.

Stanza 10 further explores the lady's spirit, suggesting that her basic motives are negative. She looks to heaven because she disdains earth; she sits high because she hates lowliness. Then, in an ambiguous image, Spenser tells us that ''underneath her scorneful feete, was laine / A dreadfull Dragon.'' The lady supposes this indicates her disdain for all the dragon represents; it also suggests that her being is firmly planted on the dragon's back. Scorn, hate, disdain—these, together with fear and jealousy, are the passions that drive her, and yet the baseness she scorns is the foundation of her life. Stanza 10 concludes with an image of her blinding self-involvement: ''And in her hand she held a mirrhour bright, / Wherein her face she often vewed faine, / And in her selfe-lov'd semblance tooke delight.'' She loves the image her mirror shows, but we understand that, on a deeper level, she hates herself.

Stanza ll reveals the lady's parents, Pluto and Proserpina, the king and queen of hell. Seated high and shining like a sun, she actually springs from the deepest and darkest of places, and the futility of her life is that her desperate attempts to escape her nature only confirm it. She repudiates her parents' lowness and claims high Jove as her father, but her very aspirations refute her claim, for, as Spenser adds, "if that any else did Jove excell" she would claim him. Her desires have no goal and consequently no possibility of satisfaction: she does not really seek to move toward anything but only away from what she disdains.

The lady's nature, we have learned, is diabolic—in her restless energy she looks forward to Milton's Satan—and now in stanza 12 Spenser concludes by giving her the name that summarizes what we have already discovered: she is Lucifera, "bearer of light," or, with less irony, a female Lucifer, Satan in a jeweled gown. Like Satan, Lucifera represents lawless will. She has no authority for her crown other than her own will, and she rules not "with lawes, but pollicie."

Miserable herself, Lucifera is the guiding spirit for a joylesss court of backbiters who spend their time competing in physical vanities, arranging their hair and clothes, sneering at each other's pride. One would hardly expect this queen to welcome newcomers warmly, and her reception of Redcross and Duessa is appropriately wretched: "With loftie eyes, halfe loth to looke so low, / She thanked them in her disdainefull wise, / Ne other grace vouchsafed them to show" (iv.14). In every sense, Lucifera's is an uncivil court. The House of Pride may be a place where men gather, but, dazzling as it is in material splendor, it is finally at least as lonely and savage as the depths of the wilderness.

After the knight's and lady's introduction, the courtiers fawn upon them, paying special attention to Duessa, whom they already know. Redcross, however, remains aloof. The "stout Faerie," Spenser tells us, "Thought all their glorie vaine in knightly vew, / And that great Princesse too exceeding prowd, / That to strange knight no better countenance allowd" (iv.15). The knight's instincts are good, he perceives the shallowness of this court. Yet we must not miss the suggestion that Redcross' aloofness is a form of pique: his vanity has been wounded in not being welcomed by Lucifera with the honor he believes he deserves. The young man, ushered into the court by a servant named Vanity, is not, after all, entirely out of his element in Lucifera's house, and his aloofness emphasizes how much he and Lucifera, both trapped in the material world of appearances, have in common.

Canto IV consists of three segments, the introductory description of the palace and its mistress; the procession of deadly sins, which forms a kind of centerpiece; and the introduction of Sansjoy. The procession begins with an abruptness that reflects Lucifera's unregulated spirit, the willfulness with which she runs her court. Like any bored, dissatisfied person, Lucifera is subject to unpredictable changes of mood:

Suddein upriseth from her stately place

> The royall Dame, and for her coche doth call:
> All hurtlen forth, and she with Princely pace,
> As faire Aurora in her purple pall.
> Out of the East the dawning day doth call:
> So forth she comes: her brightnesse brode doth
>   blaze;
> The heapes of people thronging in the hall,
> Do ride each other, upon her to gaze:
> Her glorious glitterand light doth all men eyes
>   amaze.   (iv.16)

The comparison of Lucifera to Aurora, the dawn, plays upon her name, recapitulating the light imagery with which she was first presented, but of course the image is ironic, and the passage concludes with an emphatically placed pun on "amaze," recalling the labyrinth of the wandering wood. Yet in a different sense the evocation of Aurora is appropriate at this point, for the passage does herald the coming of light, the revelation to us of the court's real ugliness in the counselors' grotesque procession.

Lucifera has six counselors, Idleness, Gluttony, Lechery, Avarice, Envy, and Wrath: the last of the traditional deadly sins is of course Pride, the root of the others, Lucifera herself. Spenser thus in effect labels Lucifera, but we should notice that her metamorphosis into an abstraction comes after her concrete realization as a proud, unhappy lady. The abstract label naturally does not replace the earlier portrait but complements it, adding to our understanding both of Pride and of who and what the lady is.

Spenser's description of the procession is conspicuously patterned, each sin receiving precisely three stanzas. This controlled surface, analogous to the superficial beauty and order of Lucifera's court, only emphasizes the bizarre disorder of the procession, the inner chaos of the House of Pride, and the counselors' utter lack of inner control. Lucifera's coach is "drawne of six unequall beasts, / On which her six sage Counsellours did ride, / Taught to obay their bestiall beheasts" (iv.18). The grammatical ambiguity is humorous: who is obeying whom? The pairing of teams is also humorous: Idleness on an ass paired with Gluttony on a swine, Lechery on a goat with Avarice on a camel, Envy on a wolf with Wrath on a lion. What a ride this coach and six must give! Although the procession is explicitly allegorical and thus intellectual in its appeal, our primary response is in fact to the comic grotesqueness of the spectacle and to the repulsiveness of these deformed creatures, all of them diseased and wretchedly unhappy. The effect is of a weird phantasmagoria spinning by while we, like Redcross, remain stationary. Sin is in bouncing, bumping motion but the knight, significantly, is going nowhere; his spiritual progress has stopped.

We should notice how the procession develops themes and motifs introduced earlier. Avarice, for example, is a materialist and as a result, like Lucifera, insatiable: "Most wretched wight, whom nothing might suffise" (iv.29). Fire imagery is pervasive: Gluttony's internal heat, which makes it impossible for him to wear human garments, Lechery's burning heart, and Wrath's fiery brand and burning eyes all comment upon Lucifera's blazing, encouraging us to consider more fully this aspect of her brilliance. We should note, too, the way the procession alludes to aspects of Redcross' career. Idleness, so "drownd in sleepe" that he "knew not, whether right he went, or else astray" (iv.19), mirrors Redcross' obliviousness, as does Gluttony, so "drowned" in sensuality that "from his friend he seldome knew his fo" (iv.23). And Lechery is, of course, like Redcross, inconstant.

The final figure in the progress is, appropriately, Satan, whipping on the team, and the unhappy procession is surrounded by a crowd, "showting for joy":

> . . . and still before their way
> A foggy mist had covered all the land;
> And underneath their feet, all scattered lay
> Dead sculs and bones of men, whose life had
> gone astray.   (iv.36)

This is the palace park viewed absolutely, an ossuary shrouded in fog, symbolizing the blindness that leads to death. Yet the next stanza abruptly shifts in perspective as Spenser, concluding the episode, reminds us how the same landscape appears to those who do not realize that their vision is dim:

> So forth they marchen in this goodly sort,
> To take the solace of the open aire,
> And in fresh flowring fields themselves to sport;
> Emongst the rest rode that false Lady faire,
> The fowle Duessa, next unto the chaire
> Of proud Lucifera, as one of the traine:
> But that good knight would not so nigh repaire,
> Him selfe estraunging from their joyaunce vaine,
> Whose fellowship seemd far unfit for warlike swaine.
>   (iv.37)

The "good knight" keeps his distance, but the episode has suggested that he perhaps has more in "fellowship" with these counselors than he understands.

The last segment introduces Sansjoy, the third Saracen brother, and an appropriate figure to find in this joyless house. All through the canto Redcross has stood aloof, unconscious of his own connection with Lucifera and her court, just as earlier he refused to recognize his brotherhood with Fradubio. But the possessor of the shield of Sansfoy cannot forever remain uninvolved, and in the final episode Redcross is directly challenged by Sansjoy. The young man is of course determined to retain Sansfoy's shield, which he considers a sign of honor, but as the battle begins Lucifera intervenes, insisting that the contest be conducted in formal lists the next day. The knights consent, passing the evening in a feast served by Gluttony until at last Sloth calls them to rest. But Sansjoy, thinking about revenge, cannot sleep, and before the canto ends Duessa proves her duplicity by visiting the pagan, assuring him that by right both she and the shield belong to him rather than Redcross—as indeed they do, in another sense as well—and encouraging him to avenge his brother's death.

Canto V

Canto IV concludes with Sansjoy's insomnia before battle as he meditates revenge; canto V begins with Redcross' wakefulness through the same night, but the Christian is more positively occupied, planning how to win honor in the coming fight. One of the points of the contrast that links the cantos is the joylessness of the Saracen's grim code of honor. As I suggested earlier, most of Spenser's characters are well-intentioned: the same passions—desire for love, for honor, for happiness—drive the wicked and the virtuous, for the problem of evil in his world, as in Plato's, is not so much a matter of motive as of knowledge. Sansjoy is actually a rather dignified character, sincere and brave; but to be a pagan is, for Spenser, to be imprisoned in the kind of hopeless pattern of life represented by the code of revenge. Such men may attain tragic dignity in Spenser, but, as Sansjoy's name implies, happiness they will never find.

Sansjoy was introduced as a man who "seemd in hart to harbour thoughts unkind" (iv.38), and Spenser echoes this phrase with significant changes in the initial stanza of canto V:

> The noble hart, that harbours vertuous thought,
> And is with child of glorious great intent,
> Can never rest, untill it forth have brought
> Th'eternall brood of glorie excellent:
> Such restlesse passion did all night torment

> The flaming corage of that Faery knight,
> Devizing, how that doughtie turnament
> With greatest honour he atchieven might;
> Still did he wake, and still did watch for dawning
>   light.   (v.1)

Focusing on the restlessness of the "noble hart," this stanza casts the preceding canto in a new light by revealing the noble ambition which, as we can now see, Lucifera's restless aspiration only parodies. The pregnancy metaphor affirms the naturalness, the fundamental healthiness, of virtuous aspiration, the results of which are very different from those of Lucifera's efforts: the glories of her court are subject to time and decay, but the children of the noble heart are an "eternall brood."

"Eternall brood"—the phrase recalls that other swarm of progeny, Error's brood. Parody is one of Spenser's most important devices for shaping his poem: the waters of lust parody the waters of life, the tree in which Fradubio is imprisoned parodies the tree of life, the House of Pride, as we shall see, parodies the House of Holiness. Normally, Spenser introduces us first to perversity then to healthiness: reading the poem thus becomes, like history itself in the Christian view, a form of gradual revelation, the parodic images foreshadowing the truth that follows. As we read we are being educated in stages, led to know good, as Milton put it, by discovering evil. Moreover, the parodic technique emphasizes the apparent similarity between evil and good, so much alike and yet so different, helping us to appreciate how easily a young man like Redcross can mistake the false for the true.

The initial part of stanza 1 is a general description of virtuous striving; the latter part presents Redcross as an example, assuring us that his restless passion is noble. But this latter part is more ambiguous than it first appears. Redcross' "flaming corage"—that is, flaming heart—uncomfortably recalls Lechery's burning heart and also the image of Phaethon's blazing fall. Redcross is planning how to win the greatest possible honor, but in this tournament, fought under the presidency of pride for Duessa and the shield of faithlessness, is there any way of achieving genuine honor? In more than one sense the knight is still waiting for the dawning light.

Though the key to virtue is knowledge, we are all ignorant at first. Indeed, the pregnancy metaphor implies that knowledge, like all "glorie excellent," is born with painful labor. The sign of churlishness is the failure to learn, to keep moving and growing: for all her restlessness, Lucifera is really as trapped, as immobile, as Fradubio. The mark of the noble heart is that it can never rest. Redcross is now in the House of Pride, but the young man is not destined to stop forever in this court, and in fact his labors here will prove to be part of the pains of birth.

In stanza 2, fusing classical mythology and the language of the Psalms, Spenser describes the sun, Phoebus Apollo, joyously "daucing forth" like a "bridegrome to his mate," and then portrays Redcross arming for the battle. Again the implications of the imagery are ambiguous. The knight's "sun-bright armes" suggest that he is a kind of earthly Apollo, but we can recall the "litle glooming light" that his armor gave in

the Error episode and wonder whether he is really
Phoebus or only the presumptuous Phaethon. Moreover, unlike Apollo, Redcross does not emerge a
bridegroom—he has abandoned his mate long since—
but only steps forth into the ''commune hall'' of the
House of Pride, where minstrels are employed to dis-
perse the sadness of the court.

Throughout the story Spenser has kept us conscious of
his presence as the poet, and we should note how the
description of Lucifera's artists reinforces his authority
by implicity contrasting his purposes as a moral teacher
with theirs.

> There many Minstrales maken melody,
> To drive away the dull melancholy,
> And many Bardes, that to the trembling
>   chord
> Can tune their timely voices cunningly,
> And many Chroniclers, that can record
> Old loves, and warres for Ladies doen by many a lord.
>   (v.3)

Lucifera's minstrels are merely entertainers: yet in a
larger sense, driving away sadness is Spenser's purpose
too. Her bards with their ''timely voices''—''timely'' is
of course a pun—are merely servants of the moment. But
Spenser's voice, rich in archaisms, is conspicuously
untimely: he sings for Elizabeth rather than Lucifera
and his song, as we know from the poem, comes from
the antique rolls of Gloriana's ''everlasting scrine.''
Moreover, Lucifera's chroniclers only ''record / Old
loves, and warres,'' a phrase that recalls and
significantly contrasts with Spenser's assertion in the

proem that "Fierce warres and faithfull loves shall moralize my song."

The Saracen enters, Lucifera is seated on her throne, and with a musical flourish that makes us think of the angels blowing forth Judgment Day—"A shrilling trumpet sownded from on hie"—the battle begins. Stanza 7 insists upon the fundamental differences between the pagan, fighting for revenge, and the Christian, fighting for honor:

> The Sarazin was stout, and wondrous strong,
>   And heaped blowes like iron hammers great:
>   For after bloud and vengeance he did long.
>   The knight was fiers, and full of youthly heat:
>   And doubled strokes, like dreaded thunders threat:
>   For all for praise and honour he did fight.
>   Both stricken strike, and beaten both do beat,
>   That from their shields forth flieth firie light,
> And helmets hewen deepe, shew marks of eithers
>   might.   (v.7)

The final lines stress the battle's ferocity and the knights' equivalent powers, but every detail in the first six symmetrically balanced lines emphasizes the contrast between the contestants; note, for example, the association of the pagan with Vulcan's weapon, the hammer, while the Christian fights with blows like the sky king's thunder.

In stanza 8 the contrast is put in moral terms as the tournament becomes a contest of absolute good against evil:

> So th'one for wrong, the other strives for right:
>   As when a Grifon seized of his pray,

A Dragon fiers encountreth in his flight,
Through widest aire making his idle way,
That would his rightfull ravine rend away:
With hideous horrour both together smight,
And souce so sore, that they the heavens affray:
The wise Southsayer seeing so sad sight,
Th'amazed vulgar tels of warres and mortall
fight.   (v.8)

The simile of the dragon and griffon fighting in the air
may be confusing; the comparison of the pagan to the
dragon perhaps gives us no trouble, but that of the
Christian to the griffon surely does unless we know that
the griffon was long a symbol for Christ. Once again,
then, there are hints of Judgment Day, when evil is
supposed to be finally overthrown, and also, especially
in the last three lines, hints of the civil war in heaven.
The apocalyptic overtones draw us into Redcross' view of
this battle—he regards himself as the embodiment of
good—but they must seem rather inappropriate when we
remember before whose throne he is fighting and what
his "rightfull ravine" is. Indeed, the description of the
battle also contains hints that, no matter how different
the professed faiths are, the two men are really much the
same. Their forces are equivalent, as we have seen.
Moreover, though the griffon may be a symbol for
Christ, the simile can also be read as suggesting merely a
fight between monsters, a "sad sight" that affrays the
heavens in a sense much more humble than the apoca-
lptic. In many ways the struggle is what Spenser calls it
in stanza 11, a "doubtfull battell."

Spying his dead brother's shield, Sansjoy doubles his
ire and, preparing to give the death blow, delivers a tri-

umphant speech in the pagan heroic tradition (it echoes
Pyrrhus' address to Priam just before he kills him to
avenge Achilles in the *Aeneid*), telling Redcross to take
a message to Sansfoy in the underworld that his brother
has won back his shield. The blow sends Redcross
reeling, and Duessa, thinking the contest nearly over,
encourages the pagan by shouting, ''Thine the shield,
and I, and all'' (v. 11). Redcross, however, assumes the
encouragement is meant for him and suddenly wakes
from his ''swowning dreame.'' ''Quickning faith, that
earst was woxen weake,'' the knight gathers his forces:
''Of all attonce he cast avengd to bee'' (v. 12). Comic
and sad, this confused moment—we should not miss
the sly humor of the placement of Redcross' mistake
immediately after the battle is termed ''doubtfull''—
ironically echoes the fight with Error when at a similarly
crucial point Una cried, ''Now now Sir knight, shew
what ye bee, / Add faith unto your force, and be not
faint'' (i. 19). Once again Redcross' revival of faith, this
time faith in faithless Duessa, shows what he is: no
longer fighting for honor—he has awakened from that
''swowning dreame'' of apocalyptic glory—he is merely,
like the pagan, seeking revenge. Driving Sansjoy to his
knees, Redcross delivers his own triumphant speech of
vengeance, telling the pagan to bear his message to
Sansfoy: ''Goe say, his foe thy shield with his doth
beare'' (v. 13). The knight has said more than he
realizes. At this moment a ''darkesome clowd''—the
image has a long history in epic, going back to the *Iliad*,
but it is particularly appropriate here as a reflection of
Redcross' intellectual limitations—descends upon

Sansjoy and the Saracen disappears. Redcross is left alone on the field, the upholder now of joylessness as well as the possessor of Sansfoy's shield.

Duessa rushes to Redcross and, confirming that he has won, advises him to "quench the flame of furious despight, / And bloudie vengeance" (v. 14). Still "amazed," the knight walks to Lucifera's throne, "And falling her before on lowly knee, / To her makes present of his service seene" (v. 16). Earlier he stood aloof, but now Redcross has become a full-fledged member of Lucifera's court, her servant rather than Gloriana's. Lucifera praises what Spenser ironically calls the knight's "gay chevalree" and her courtiers escort him home joyously. But the final image is of Redcross lying in "griefe and agony" in the sumptuousness of his hero's bed; surrounded by honor and riches, he is nevertheless as wretched as Lucifera herself. "And all the while," Spenser tells us, Duessa, sitting by his bed, "wept full bitterly" (v. 17). Yet her grief is as superficial as his joy, and in stanza 18 Spenser gives us an extended simile that compares her weeping to a crocodile's tears:

As when a wearie traveler that strayes
   By muddy shore of broad seven-mouthed Nile,
   Unweeting of the perilous wandring wayes,
   Doth meet a cruell craftie Crocodile,
   Which in false griefe hiding his harmefull guile,
   Doth weepe full sore, and sheddeth tender teares:
   The foolish man, that pitties all this while
   His mournefull plight, is swallowed up unwares,
Forgetfull of his owne, that mindes anothers cares.
(v.18)

Recalling the earlier comparison of Error's vomit to the

Nile's overflowing, the simile reminds us that we are still in Egypt and far from the Promised Land. The Nile simile also provides the link between the tournament and the canto's second episode, Duessa's descent to hell to secure help for Sansjoy, preparing for the grief we are about to witness in the underworld by warning against too great pity lest we, too, be "swallowd up unwares."

Canto V moves from the brightness of the tournament to the darkness of Night's cave and the descent through Avernus to hell. The episode begins as Duessa, shining with jewels, seeks out Night, who at first fails to recognize her granddaughter and, frightened by Duessa's brightness, tries to retreat into her cave. The image parodies Redcross at the cave of Error, but whereas he was able to peer only a little way into the darkness, we are now about to penetrate to the depths. Despite Duessa's apparent brightness, Night is her grandmother, the "root" of her race, just as Lucifera comes from Pluto and Proserpina. In the underworld episode we are, in effect, exploring the dark foundations of the glittering House of Pride, examining the core of Lucifera's being as well as Duessa's. Duessa's journey also recalls that earlier episode modeled on the descent tradition of the classical epics, Archimago's embassy to Morpheus in canto I, but there Spenser's emphasis was upon the demonic, here it is upon ignorance—for the dominant theme of canto V is the sad benightedness of the pagan world.

From the beginning, the underworld episode is conspicuously classical, conspicuously pagan. We should note, for instance, the parody of heroic rhetoric with which Duessa addresses Night, recounting the goddess' honors and bidding her avenge the injury done her race in the defeat of Sansfoy and Sansjoy. Night responds with stoic dignity. She grieves for the fall of these "famous children,"

> But who can turne the streame of destinee,
> Or breake the chaine of strong necessitee,
> Which fast is tide to Joves eternall seat?
> The sonnes of Day he favoureth, I see,
> And by my ruines thinkes to make them great:
> To make one great by others losse, is bad excheat.
>
> (v.25)

Night promises that Redcross will suffer for the blood he has spilled, but her view of things is essentially without hope: Jove has ultimate power and he favors the sons of Day. No reason for Jove's antipathy is given, for she can imagine none; the universe, as she views it, is lawless, run simply by will and power. Spenser is asking us to look for a moment through Night's eyes and appreciate how the world appears to the unenlightened, but any temptation to sympathize too deeply is thwarted by comedy when Duessa with absurd pride identifies herself as the daughter of Deceit and Shame, names that are to her genuinely heroic.

Duessa and Night retrieve Sansjoy and carry him to the "yawning gulfe of deepe Avernus hole" (v. 31), the traditional entrance to the underworld in classical literature. Spenser has warned us of the danger of being "swallowd up," and now this warning becomes especially relevant as we enter the mouth of hell. Penetrating deeper and deeper into a realm of monsters and souls in torment, we come at last to the "furthest part," the deepest place in hell, "Where was a Cave ywrought by wondrous art, / Deepe, darke, uneasie, dolefull, comfortlesse" (v. 36). The art that has created this doleful cave reflects that of the cave's resident, "sad Aesculapius," the mythological healer punished by Jove for curing Hippolytus. In stanzas 37-39 Spenser digresses from the description of Aesculapius to recount Hippolytus' story in such a way that it reminds us of Redcross, who has also, in a sense, been attacked by monsters from the sea. Like Hippolytus, Redcross needs to be put back together again—we recall that in canto II Spenser described Archimago's deception of his guests as dividing them into "double parts"—but the wholeness he requires is not physical. Aesculapius' science is ultimately, like the cave he inhabits, "comfortlesse." From Spenser's point of view Aesculapius is a mechanic rather than a doctor: he can reassemble Hippolytus' scattered parts, but he cannot make anyone "whole" because his knowledge is limited to man's physical nature. His science represents a pagan attempt to achieve corporeal immortality, a sad parody of the genuine immortality available to the enlightened. Appropriately, it is with this healer, a man unable even to cure his own wretchedness, that Night and Duessa leave Sansjoy.

Having taken care of Sansjoy as best they can, Duessa and Night return to the upper world and Night resumes her "timely race" through the heavens "whilst Phoebus pure / In westerne waves his wearie wagon did recure"

(v. 44). This final image in the descent episode evokes another kind of healing and reminds us that, for the enlightened, periodic descents can be medicinal. Moreover, this image prepares us for the last episode in the canto, the dwarf's belated but salutary discovery of the dungeon of the House of Pride, another, shallower, version of hell, and his return to inform his master of the dangers of remaining in this place. We naturally applaud Redcross' realization of what underlies Lucifera's house, but our own descent through Avernus has been to depths immeasurably greater. Thus, even as we watch the young man's horrified discovery of Lucifera's prisoners, we are ironically aware of how shallow his understanding still is.

The figures beneath Avernus—Ixion, Sisyphus, Tantalus, Tityus, Typhoeus, Theseus, and others—were mythical. Those in Lucifera's dungeon, Nebuchadnezzar, Croesus, Antiochus, Nimrod, and other examples of presumption, are historical: "A ruefull sight, as could be seene with eye" (v. 46). Spenser may be suggesting that, having actually lived, the historical figures can be understood more easily than the mythical, who, having no corporeal reality, cannot be "seene with eye." In any case, he emphasizes the grossly physical nature of these prisoners, thrown together like "carkases of beasts in butchers stall" (v. 49). But not only the wicked have wound up in this dungeon: among Lucifera's prisoners are, sadly enough, some of the most famous names in Roman history, and when Spenser catalogues them his imagery changes, evoking the architectural ruins of ancient Rome:

And in another corner wide were strowne
The antique ruines of the Romaines fall:
Great Romulus the Grandsire of them all,
Proud Tarquin, and too lordly Lentulus,
Stout Scipio, and stubborne Hanniball,
Ambitious Sylla, and sterne Marius,
High Caesar, great Pompey, and fierce Antonius.
(v. 49)

Spenser would have us understand that Lucifera's dungeon is the inevitable end of all glory founded upon the sandy hill of the material world, which, dazzling as it may for a time be, is doomed to inevitable decay.

It took a long time for the dwarf—from the beginning Spenser has portrayed him as a rather comic laggard—to discover the dungeon. Yet he has saved his master from the kind of danger that can be ''seene with eye.'' Redcross escapes from Lucifera's house through a rear gate, a ''privie Posterne,'' that leads through a ''fowle way'' and opens onto a ''donghill of dead carkases'' (v. 53). Implicit in this description is the familiar allegory of the body-castle, which emphasizes once again that Lucifera's glory is built upon the physical. Canto V began with the young man emerging from his chamber like Phoebus Apollo, clad in sun-bright arms; it ends with a humbler coming forth as the knight sneaks away through what is in effect the fundament of the House of Pride.

Canto VI

Spenser, like Shakespeare, allows his major patterns of imagery to accumulate gradually through puns, allusions, and indirect metaphors that often consist of merely a word or two employed casually, as if more by accident than design. At various points in the narrative, however, these gathering metaphorical patterns surface and become conspicuous, the effect being not unlike that pleasure of recognition when a composer, after developing fragmentary phrases, restates his entire theme in its simplest and purest form.

Starting with the pun on harbor and arbor when Redcross and Una entered the wandering wood, Spenser has been developing aspects of the metaphor of Redcross' journey as a sea voyage, an image that has gathered both heroic and religious associations, alluding to, among other things, the Hebrews' crossing of the Red Sea to find the Promised Land. All along the implicit issue has been whether the young man will be shipwrecked and drowned or reach port safely, and now, in the emphatic position of the first stanza of canto VI, Spenser recapitulates this theme, redefining the adventures in the House of Pride in terms of his continuing metaphor:

As when a ship, that flies faire under saile,
    An hidden rocke escaped hath unwares,
    That lay in waite her wrack for to bewaile,
    The Marriner yet halfe amazed stares
    At perill past, and yet in doubt ne dares

To joy at his foole-happie oversight:
So doubly is distrest twixt joy and cares
The dreadlesse courage of this Elfin knight,
Having escapt so sad ensamples in his sight.   (vi.1)

The simile dwells upon the mariner's lack of awareness:
believing he was in safe water, he was traveling under
full sail and only appreciated the danger when it was
past. Like Redcross, who never saw more than the tip of
the rock upon which he nearly foundered, the mariner
escapes shipwreck more by luck than skill.

Although Redcross is pleased to have escaped the
"sad ensamples" of the House of Pride, he has not
found joy. Ironically, he is still himself a sad example—
through repetition, "sad" has by now become a symbolic term—mistakenly grieved to have left Duessa behind, and "yet more sad, that Una his deare dreed /
Her truth had staind with treason so unkind" (vi.2).

Spenser now turns to his principal subject in canto VI,
Una, picking up her story where canto III left off. Sansloy
has carried Una into a "forest wilde"—this forest is the
key to the structure of canto VI, which will be concerned
with how Una gets out of the woods—and is about to
rape her when "providence," Spenser tells us, finds an
unexpected way to rescue her from "Lions clawes" (vi.7).
The lion of the metaphor is Sansloy, which at first may
seem inappropriate since the last time we saw Una a lion
was her defender. And yet the comparison is significant,
for Una's rescuers, the "salvage nation" of fauns and
satyrs (creatures half-animal, half-human) not only save
her from Sansloy but also, in replacing the lion as her
defender, deliver her from pure bestiality, carrying her
some way toward the human.

Though a step above the lion in the hierarchy of being, the fauns and satyrs are, nevertheless, forest dwellers. In canto III, when the lion demonstrated his gentleness, Spenser employed an image to suggest the specifically subhuman responding sympathetically to Una's plight, describing how her cries "softly ecchoed from the neighbour wood" (iii.8), and now, introducing the salvage nation, he uses a variant of the same formula:

> Her shrill outcries and shriekes so loud did bray,
> That all the woodes and forestes did resownd;
> A troupe of Faunes and Satyres far away
> Within the wood were dauncing in a rownd,
> Whiles old Sylvanus slept in shady arber sownd. (vi.7)

The circle dance suggests the creatures' self-sufficiency, and we should also note the grammatical ambiguity in the final line. Does "sownd" modify the forest god's sleep, or does it imply that his "shady arber"—the natural world he inhabits—is unenlightened but fundamentally sound?

Hearing Una's cries, the fauns and satyrs, a "rude, misshapen, monstrous rablement" (vi.8), come running and frighten away Sansloy. Once again Spenser reminds us of the lion in canto III by comparing the "wild wood-gods" to a lion that frightens away a wolf about to devour a lamb. Like that lion, the fauns and satyrs prove gentle, and, instead of attacking Una, they prostrate themselves before her, kissing her feet. Yet, friendly as the forest creatures are, they are spiritually perverse, as Spenser suggests when he tells us their knees are "backward bent"—he is of course playing with the image of their animal, specifically goatish, lower parts—and when, punning on truth and troth, he describes Una's initial reluctance to submit herself to "their barbarous truth" (vi.12).

Canto V was concerned with the pagan world, and canto VI, we realize, is continuing this theme in rather different terms: fauns and satyrs are of course figures from classical mythology, and Sylvanus, the salvage nation's chief, is the Roman god of fields and forests. What Spenser seems to be suggesting in their replacement of the lion as Una's guardian is a historical process, the gradual progress from a state of nature to "barbarous truth," the early and still imperfect civilization of the pagans. In canto V the pagan world was sad, but here Spenser, drawing upon the pastoral tradition and the idea of the golden age when the world was young and happy in its innocence, portrays the fauns and satyrs as "glad, as birdes of joyous Prime" (vi.13). But, though the picture of their innocent joy as they lead Una to Sylvanus is attractive, "birdes of joyous Prime" recalls the singing birds in the Wood of Error, reminding us that innocence may also be a form of ignorance.

Spenser is trying to shape a very complex response to this salvage nation. From one point of view the pagan world is young and innocent; from another it is old, a superseded culture, and this idea is embodied in "old Sylvanus"—his age associates him with a series of characters that includes, ominously, Archimago—who, hearing the fauns and satyrs approach, "commeth out, / To weet the cause, his weake steps governing, / And aged limbs on Cypresse stadle stout" (vi.14). Significantly, in his weakness Sylvanus leans upon a wooden staff, upon nature. Sylvanus is as amazed as the fauns and satyrs by Una's beauty but, whereas they are content to worship her, he attempts to comprehend what she is:

> The woodborne people fall before her flat,
>> And worship her as Goddesse of the wood;
>> And old Sylvanus selfe bethinkes not, what
>> To thinke of wight so faire, but gazing stood,
>> In doubt to deeme her borne of earthly brood;
>> Sometimes Dame Venus selfe he seemes to see,
>> But Venus never had so sober mood;
>> Sometimes Diana he her takes to bee,
> But misseth bow, and shaftes, and buskins to her knee.
>> (vi.16)

But pagan concepts, the only ones Sylvanus understands, will not serve, for Una, as loving as Venus and as chaste as Diana, represents a synthesis and transcendence of the old gods that is beyond the ancients' comprehension.

Having failed to understand Una, Sylvanus in effect resorts to his cypress prop, drifting in stanza 17 into a reverie about his "ancient love," Cypariss, who, as Spenser's readers would have known from Ovid, changed after his death into a cypress tree. Sylvanus compares the boy to Una, realizing how much more beautiful she is, and then sadly recalls how Cypariss worshipped a gentle hind: one day Sylvanus by accident killed the hind, "For griefe whereof the lad n'ould after joy, / But pind away in anguish and selfe-wild annoy." The pun on "pind" alludes to the boy's metamorphosis into a tree, and his story as a whole suggests the pathos of pagan life founded upon the fragility of nature.

Moreover, the boy's languishing contrasts with Una's heroic perserverence in adversity. "Ancient"—that is, pagan—in many different ways, this homosexual love between Cypariss and the god of forests represents for Spenser an outmoded and sad kind of love, one that has been replaced by something better.

Pleased that she is among creatures who intend her no harm, but distressed that they treat her as a goddess, Una attempts to "teach them truth." But her effort to raise the salvage nation above idolatry is as futile as Sylvanus' attempt to understand her, and the episode ends with both comedy and pathos as Spenser, developing the motif of animal worship introduced in Cypariss' story, describes how "when their bootlesse zeale she did restrain / From her own worship, they her Asse would worship fain" (vi.19).

Cypariss' metamorphosis into a tree recalls that other character imprisoned in nature, Fradubio, just as the whole setting of canto VI reminds us of the wandering wood. Having suggested how one becomes lost, Spenser now tells how one gets out of the woods. But to lead Una from the forest requires a champion superior to the salvage nation, and in stanza 20 we meet Sir Satyrane.

Spenser establishes Satyrane's character by relating his personal history. The son of a satyr and a lady—thus a step closer than the fauns and satyrs to complete humanity—Satyrane was raised in the forest by his satyr father, who taught him to be fearless:

> His trembling hand he would him force to put
> Upon the Lion and the rugged Beare,

And from the she Beares teats her whelps to teare;
And eke wild roring Buls he would him make
To tame, and ride their backes not made to beare.

(vi.24)

Innately noble and ambitious for fame, Satyrane soon
mastered all the wild beasts of the forest and left the
woods to prove his powers in the greater world of fairy-
land. However, Satyrane periodically revisits his native
woods, and it is on one of these visits that he discovers
Una teaching the satyrs "trew sacred lore." Admiring
and pitying her, he becomes Una's student—the Satyrane story is a fable of successful education—in "faith
and veritie." And on a day when, as Spenser significantly notes, the satyrs are occupied in worshipping
their forest god, doing "their service to Sylvanus old,"
Satyrane leads Una away: "So fast he carried her with
carefull paine, / That they the woods are past, and come
now to the plaine" (vi.33).

Out of the woods, Una is not yet out of difficulty, for
she still has to find Redcross, and the final episode of
canto VI begins with a reminder of Redcross' problematic condition. Traveling in search of the Christian
knight, Una and Satyrane encounter a pilgrim—Archimago again—who testifies that Redcross is dead, slain
by a pagan. Archimago's report is slanderous; nevertheless, Redcross has had a close brush with spiritual death
in the House of Pride, and even now his condition is
"sad." Una, with faith in Redcross as "the stoutest
knight, that ever wonne" (vi.39), is reluctant to believe
the pilgrim, but Satyrane, who accepts the report at face
value, plans revenge and receives directions from

Archimago about how to find the pagan Sansloy. Again at the end of canto VI we have the vengeance motif, established in canto V and associated with the sad limitations of the pagan way of life. The central part of canto VI, in which Spenser recounts Satyrane's education, deals with the nobility of Una's latest champion; the final part suggests his limitations.

The last time we saw Archimago was at the end of canto III, disguised as Redcross, and his report of Redcross' death actually alludes to his own ignominious defeat at Sansloy's hands. This reminder of canto III helps draw our attention to the parallel conclusions of the two cantos. Once again Una's champion—the lion earlier, Satyrane now—must finally test himself against Sansloy, the lawlessness loosed upon the world by Redcross' fall from faith. Satyrane, as we would expect, fares better than the lion, but though Sansloy cannot kill him, neither can he kill the Saracen. Enlightened to a degree, Satyrane is not a Christian—Spenser perhaps associates him with such wise pagans as Plato and Aristotle, men who from the Christian point of view perceived genuine but limited truths—and the fight between Una's present champion and Sansloy is still a contest between pagans. In stanza 44 Spenser emphasizes the equivalence of the contenders, comparing their mutual pursuit of ''fell revenge'' to ''two Bores with rancling malice met,'' and the canto ends indecisively with them still locked in combat. The point is that, without a champion superior even to the noble Satyrane, the struggle against Sansfoy's brother can have no end. Yet, though Satyrane cannot overcome Sansloy completely, he does prevent the Saracen from seizing Una once more and carrying her back into the forest. Our final image of the lady is of her flight from the battle with Archimago following, hoping "to bring her to her last decay" (vi.48). At the end of canto VI, then, Una has escaped the dangers of Sansloy and the forest but, once again, she is without a champion and Archimago is hot in pursuit.

Looking back on the last four cantos, we can see that they are arranged so that Una's wanderings in the wildernesses of cantos III and VI frame Redcross' experiences in the apparently civilized House of Pride. This patterning is significant. In Redcross' cantos Spenser has given us the spectacle of a corrupt culture, a city inwardly unsound because founded upon the powers of darkness. In Una's cantos, in which the lady has passed from one defender to another, each superior to the one preceding, Spenser has been concerned with the development toward a civility that is genuine because founded upon all that is sound in nature: the instinctive benevolence of the lion, the salvage nation's good will, and Satyrane's innate nobility. The process is not complete—and will not be complete until Redcross frees Una's parents in canto XII—but in demonstrating how the foundations of civility may be firmly established, Una's cantos have suggested a positive alternative to the House of Pride.

Canto VII

The midpoint is important structurally in Spenser's poem as in many Renaissance works. Canto VII brings changes of several kinds. In the first half of the story Una has searched for Redcross with no idea of his whereabouts and no certain knowledge even of whether he is alive; in canto VII the dwarf arrives with the first true news of him, and now she becomes able to help her knight in his trials. This plot development is reflected in a formal change. As we have seen—in, say, the patterned description of the deadly sins in canto IV—poetic form in Spenser is often symbolic. In the first half Una and Redcross have dwelt, as it were, in separate cantos; now, even before their literal reunion, this formal barrier is removed and Spenser joins the lovers' stories. There is also a significant change in the dramatis personae. After the midpoint the Saracen brothers, Sansfoy, Sansloy, and Sansjoy, drop from sight, and Spenser introduces a new character, Arthur, who is to be as important in the second half as they were in the first.

These changes are symptomatic of a deeper shift. Putting it rather baldly, the poem moves from a pagan first half, defined by the Saracen brothers, to a Christian second half, defined by Arthur. In cantos III and VI Spenser traced Una's champions from the benevolent lion to the noble pagan, Satyrane; now in canto VII Arthur will become her champion until Redcross is able to resume that role. Moreover, in Redcross' own story we have seen the knight develop to the limit of unaided—that is, pre-Christian—understanding, for we should not forget that, despite his faithlessness and joylessness, he has discovered the dungeon of the House of Pride. But, even though he has seen the danger of Lucifera's materialism, Redcross has still, as the first episode of canto VII makes clear, to contend with his own corrupt nature, with that inner unsoundness symbolized by the sexual passion released during the night in Archimago's hermitage. The problem is again one of knowledge: Redcross has to discover the dangers of fleshly pride. Spenser is not, in the popular sense, a puritan, preaching the eradication of sexual desire, but he does insist upon the futility of mere lust. Redcross has to learn how to incorporate his physical desires into a greater passion; he must learn how, in the fullest Christian sense, to love. And this he cannot do without help—instruction in matters beyond the reach of reason and a basic reformation of his nature. Redcross' salvation begins in canto VII when the dwarf seeing his master overcome by Orgoglio, goes off to tell his distress.

Canto VI ends with Archimago pursuing Una; canto VII opens with Duessa pursuing Redcross, whom she finds sitting by a fountain, looking disturbingly like the lustful Sansloy, who was also sitting wearily by a fountain when Satyrane encountered him at the end of canto VI. But the initial stanza of canto VII qualifies our approach to Redcross here. Spenser asks us to pity rather than condemn Redcross' condition, reminding us in imagery that recalls Error's knotty "traine" of the radical limitations of mere "earthly wit":

> What man so wise, what earthly wit so ware,
>> As to descry the crafty cunning traine,
>> By which deceipt doth maske in visour faire,
>> And cast her colours dyed deepe in graine,
>> To seeme like Truth, whose shape she well can faine,
>> And fitting gestures to purpose frame,
>> The guiltlesse man with guile to entertaine?
>> Great maistresse of her art was that false Dame,
> The false Duessa, cloked with Fidessaes name. (vii.1)

It is an unequal contest: Spenser warns us in advance that Redcross cannot be expected to triumph over Duessa.

The opening picture of Redcross at the poem's midpoint contrasts starkly with the original description in canto I. Wearied after his escape from the House of Pride and assuming that he is now out of danger, the young man has dismounted, removed his armor, and seated himself on the ground, while his steed, the emblem of his heroic spirit, feeds on "grassy forage." The noble heart, as we know from canto V, can never rest, and yet that is exactly what Redcross is doing. In escaping from the House of Pride he has gone as far as he can; now he is motionless, his heroic quest evidently ended. The knight's diet is even less nourishing than his steed's:

> He feedes upon the cooling shade, and bayes
>> His sweatie forehead in the breathing wind,
>> Which through the trembling leaves full gently playes
>> Wherein the cherefull birds of sundry kind
>> Do chaunt sweet musick, to delight his mind. (vii.3)

"Cooling shade," "bayes" (bathes), "trembling leaves," "cherefull birds"—the passage is a mosaic of established motifs that suggest how in the decline of his heroic spirit Redcross has taken refuge in the shady realm of nature. More specifically, the description recalls Redcross and Duessa taking refuge from the scorching sun in canto II at the start of the Fradubio episode, which warned about the danger of becoming trapped in nature.

Fradubio, we remember, was to be released from bondage by bathing in a "living well," an image that suggested baptism. Spenser tells us a great deal about the fountain by which Redcross is resting, and we are meant to bear Fradubio's well in mind throughout the passage. Approaching Redcross, Duessa rebukes him for leaving her behind in the House of Pride, but the lovers' quarrel is quickly resolved and soon the couple is "bathing" in what Spenser calls the "joyous shade," a phrase that is in Spenser's metaphorical language a contradiction in terms.

> Unkindness past, they gan of solace treat,
>   And bathe in pleasaunce of joyous shade,
>   Which shielded them against the boiling heat,
>   And with greene boughes decking a gloomy glade,
>   About the fountaine like a girlond made;
>   Whose bubbling wave did ever freshly well,
>   Ne ever would through fervent sommer fade:
>   The sacred Nymph, which therein wont to dwell,
> Was out of Dianes favour, as it then befell.   (vii.4)

We should note how the "joyous shade" changes into a "gloomy glade"—the rhyme reinforces the ironic juxtaposition of phrases—that crowns and, significantly, is maintained by the fountain's bubbling waters. Spenser assures us that the fountain runs through "fervent sommer," the season when brooks generally dry up, but at another, less literal, level of meaning—perhaps "sommer" suggests the seasons of life—he seems to hint that this spring does ultimately "fade." Water and bathing are erotic motifs in Spenser's poem, and the image of the welling fountain covered by a glade of vegetation is probably, among other things, an anatomical allusion. In any case, like Fradubio's "living well," the fountain is alive, but its spirit, a classical nymph, is pagan rather than Christian. Moreover, given the erotic associations gathering about the fountain, we should not be surprised to learn that the nymph is out of favor with the goddess of chastity.

Stanza 5 explains how the nymph fell from grace. One day, weary of the heat, she "Sat downe to rest in middest of the race," and Diana angrily proclaimed that thenceforth her waters would be "dull and slow" and that anyone who drank from her would "faint and feeble grow." The mythic form of this little Ovidian fable is significant, for myths are, as we noted in connection with the underworld episode in canto V, the repositories of a kind of truth that cannot be "seene with eye." In appearance the fountain bubbles freshly, but stanza 5 reveals that it is actually feeble. Far from possessing the power to refresh Redcross, the nymph is the mirror of his lassitude.

The relationship between the knight and the disgraced spirit reminds us that the dark realm of nature into which Redcross has lapsed is as much internal as it is external. The relationship becomes even closer in stanza 6 when Redcross in effect becomes the nymph as, ignorantly drinking from her stream, his "manly forces" fail and he metaphorically liquefies—turning cold and sluggish with a diseased chill that Spenser compares to a fever. At the start of stanza 7, making "goodly court" to Duessa, he reaches a liquid sexual climax, "Pourd out in loosnesse on the grassy grownd, / Both careless of his health, and of his fame." Like old father Nilus swelling with pride in the crucial simile in canto I, Redcross has overflowed.

At this climactic moment a giant suddenly appears, "horrible and hye, / That with his talnesse seemd to threat the skye" (vii.8). A phrase like "to threat the skye" has of course more than casual meaning in Spenser. So far the action of canto VII has been sexually charged, and Spenser maintains the generally sexual atmosphere in stanza 9 when he pauses to describe the giant's origins. Parodying the account of the Virgin's impregnation by the Holy Spirit and drawing upon the established earth and cave motifs, Spenser tells how Aeolus, the wind god, impregnated Earth who, deep in her hidden caves, conceived and finally brought forth "this monstrous masse of earthly slime, / Puft up with emptie wind, and fild with sinfull crime."

> So growen great through arrogant delight
> Of th'high descent, whereof he was yborne,
> And through presumption of his matchlesse might,
> All other powres and knighthood he did scorne.
>
> (vii.10)

Like Lucifera, the giant is arrogant, proud, and scornful, but whereas her style was elaborate and elegant, a parody of civilization, Spenser emphasizes the giant's primitiveness. The product of brute nature, conceived in a cave like some Elizabethan version of Neanderthal Man, the savage monster stalks his prey through the forest while leaning upon a "snaggy Oke, which he had torne / Out of his mothers bowelles" (vii.10). The picture of the giant supporting himself upon this crude staff recalls old Sylvanus leaning upon his cypress; but, as we may remember from the catalogue of trees, the cypress is associated with funerals, and the image of Sylvanus, still mourning his dead Cypariss, was a sad picture of weakness. The "builder Oake," on the other hand, is "sole king of forrests all" (i.8), and the giant, too, is a kind of savage king, employing his oak not merely as a staff but as a mace, both the emblem of his authority and his weapon.

The key to the giant's import is the moment of his appearance. His bellowing approach is heard in the same stanza that describes Redcross and Duessa sprawled in "loosnesse" on the ground, and indeed his arrival is part of the climax of their erotic encounter. Primitive and brutal, a puffed-up mass of earth that later collapses like a bladder when the air is released—Renaissance physiology understood male erection to be caused by air rather than blood—this monster, like the welling fountain, is anatomically suggestive, a kind of ambulatory male member. When the monster appears Redcross, deep in erotic play, is disarmed, unable to resist, and so feeble from the nymph's waters that when the giant attacks with his phallic mace he is overcome merely by the wind of the blow.

Only after the giant's barbaric character has been

vividly established, and Redcross defeated, does Spenser almost casually reveal his name: Orgoglio—that is, in Italian, pride. "Pride" has sexual connotations as we have seen, but many other meanings as well. The name Orgoglio confirms the anatomical allusion, but at the same time enlarges the giant's significance, reminding us that Redcross' uncontrolled erotic impulses are themselves only symbolic of the larger problem of human nature as Spenser conceives it, the difficulty of the immortal spirit imprisoned in a "mass of earthly slime." Carried off to rot in Orgoglio's dungeon, Redcross is, like Fradubio imprisoned in his tree, trapped in his own physical nature.

Duessa, however, flourishes, for Orgoglio lavishes honors upon her, dressing her in gold and purple and setting her upon a seven-headed dragon. It is useful to know that this description of Duessa in her glory identifies her with the Whore of Babylon and that sixteenth-century Protestants often associated the Whore with the Roman Church. Yet, even without background knowledge, the general import of Duessa's prospering as Redcross languishes is clear. Moreover, the image of her astride the seven-headed beast recalls Lucifera standing upon a dragon and reaches back to the initial image of Error, the monster with a woman's head. We should note, too, that Spenser compares this beast to "that renowmed Snake / Which great Alcides in Stremona slew" (vii.17), reminding us at the end of the Orgoglio episode that monsters, no matter how terrible, can be slain.

The second part of canto VII, moving from despair to hope, shifts our attention to Una. The pivotal figure is the dwarf—the ironic humor implicit in the contrast between the dwarf and the giant is obvious and effective—who brings Una word of her knight. But before the dwarf can speak, Una, assuming Redcross is dead, faints, recovering only long enough to deliver a despairing lament before fainting again. The effect of Una's momentary despair is positive, for we know—and she very soon learns—that Redcross still lives: Spenser has organized his material to emphasize that, dire as they are, Redcross' circumstances are not hopeless. This brief episode provides the emotional transition between the gloom of the first part of the canto, the Orgoglio episode, and the joyous description of Arthur that follows.

A general word about Spenser's narrative technique may be useful here. In the modern narratives to which we are accustomed, principally novels, there are few if any long, formal descriptions of characters and places. Contemporary writers normally try to keep such "undramatic" material to the minimum. At the very least they attempt to avoid long, unbroken stretches of inert matter by mixing what description their story requires with liberal doses of dialogue. In Spenser, on the other hand, there is a great deal of formal description. Characters and important locales are normally described in detail when first introduced, and there are also the detailed similes and such "set pieces" as the description of the deadly sins. In complete contrast with modern novels, the descriptions in Spenser are not only often the most complex and interesting parts of the narrative, but frequently the most dramatic as well because Spenser's allusive technique, his method of employing ironic echoes of earlier images and motifs, permits him to charge his descriptions with dramatic conflict. Moreover, Spenser's descriptions are rarely reducible to static portraits that might be taken in at a glance; rather, they tend to be gradual, progressive revelations of character and theme which serve a dynamic function not unlike the novelist's dialogue. Arthur's appearance in canto VII is perhaps the major turning point of the poem. At this moment a novelist would invent a scene, an action. Spenser gives us an elaborate description of Arthur's armor.

The description begins in stanza 29 as Una is traveling with her dwarf:

> At last she chaunced by good hap to meet
>> A goodly knight, faire marching by the way
>> Together with his Squire, arayed meet:
>> His glitterand armour shined farre away,
>> Like glauncing light of Phoebus brightest ray;
>> From top to toe no place appeared bare,
>> That deadly dint of steele endanger may:
>> Athwart his brest a bauldrick brave he ware,
> That shind, like twinkling stars, with stons most
>> pretious rare.   (vii.29)

From the first, Spenser's diction carefully controls our response to this new figure: Una, for example, does not merely meet Arthur, she meets him "by good hap." What is remarkable, however, is not merely the number of positive terms in the opening lines—"good hap," "goodly knight," "faire marching," "arayed meet"— but the fact that they are presented without the usual qualifiers, such as "seemed." In a poem so pervasively ironic the sudden absence of even a hint of irony is dramatic. We should note, too, the movement in the last six lines. Initially we seem to see Arthur from a great distance—"His glitterand armour shined farre away"— like a ray of hope on the horizon of our understanding. Soon, though, he has come close enough for us to have a general picture of him, armed without gap from head to toe, an image that contrasts sharply with Redcross at the start of the canto, disarmed and unprepared for Orgoglio's attack. And, finally, we can even distinguish the gemstones on his baldric, shining like "twinkling stars." The method of describing Arthur's armor rather than his "self" is significant, recalling the initial presentation of Redcross in canto I. In Arthur's case, however, there is no sense of disparity between the man and his exterior, for Arthur, in a sense, is his armor: he is the fully realized knight that Redcross must still become.

The governing image of stanza 29 is of an approaching light. Lucifera, too, was presented largely in terms of light, and in stanza 30 the allusion becomes more explicit as Spenser focuses on the centerpiece of Arthur's jeweled baldric, where a "pretious stone / Of wondrous worth, and eke of wondrous mights, / Shapt like a Ladies head, exceeding shone, / Like Hesperus emongst the lesser lights." (The key phrase "exceeding shone" will be repeated a few stanzas later in the description of Arthur's shield.) Yet Arthur's effect, in contrast with Lucifera's, is of shining rather than blazing light, and we may remember the important line from the Phaethon simile describing the presumptuous youth's blazing fall, lighting the sky with "fire not made to burne, but fairely for to shine" (iv.9). In its new context the phrase "exceeding shone" has been wholly transformed in connotation, now suggesting a wonder, a miracle—the precise significance of the lady's head, however, remains mysterious until later when we learn that Arthur is in love with Gloriana. Earlier, in connection with Lucifera, it signified a dangerous lack of control.

The recollection of Lucifera is the first in a series of allusions to negative motifs that are transformed into positive signs, suggesting that the knight's fulfilled glory is built not upon a rejection but an incorporation and metamorphosis of human nature. Stanzas 31 and 32 describe Arthur's helmet, carrying the eye progressively higher in an upward movement that is itself symbolic and that concludes, significantly, with a reference to heaven:

> His haughtie helmet, horrid all with gold,
>> Both glorious brightnesse, and great terrour bred;
>> For all the crest a Dragon did enfold
>> With greedie pawes, and over all did spred
>> His golden wings: his dreadfull hideous hed
>> Close couched on the bever, seem'd to throw
>> From flaming mouth bright sparkles fierie red,
>> That suddeine horror to faint harts did show;
> And scaly taile was stretcht adowne his backe full low.

> Upon the top of all his loftie crest,
>> A bunch of haires discolourd diversly,
>> With sprincled pearle, and gold full richly drest,
>> Did shake, and seem'd to daunce for jollity,
>> Like to an Almond tree ymounted hye,
>> On top of greene Selinis all alone,

With bloosomes brave bedecked daintily;
Whose tender locks do tremble every one
At every little breath, that under heaven is blowne.

(vii.31-32)

The dragon of stanza 31 inevitably recalls the poem's earlier monsters; yet the dragon was the symbol of the Welsh ruler, the Pendragon—Arthur is of course a Welsh prince, the son of Uther Pendragon—and in this context the monster's hideousness, sending "suddeine horror to faint harts," becomes the emblem of Arthur's power. Moreover, fearsome as it is, the dragon yields as the description progresses to the "bunch of haires discolourd diversly." This phrase is repeated word for word from canto II where Spenser described Archimago, disguised as Redcross, as having "on his craven crest / A bounch of haires discolourd diversly" (ii.11). In its original context "discolourd" possessed negative connotations, but in the description of Arthur's crest Spenser develops an image of gay variegation, adding pearl and gold, and telling us that the plume "Did shake and seem'd to daunce for jollity," a line that delicately recalls the joyous image of dawn in canto V when "Phoebus fresh, as bridegrome to his mate, / Came daun`cing forth, shaking his deawie haire" (v.2). Furthermore, in the simile that completes the description, the brush becomes a triumphant, high-mounted almond tree—it may help to know that the almond, a tree not included in the canto I catalogue, is often used as a symbol of life and renewal—with "tender locks" that tremble at heaven's breath, an image that transforms the "trembling" motif introduced in the Fradubio episode from a sign of fear to one of responsiveness to divine will.

Stanzas 33-36 describe Arthur's miraculous diamond shield which he keeps covered except when he uses it as a weapon, defeating his foes with its light:

> For so exceeding shone his glistring ray,
> That Phoebus golden face it did attaint,
> As when a cloud his beames doth over-lay;
> And silver Cynthia wexed pale and faint,
> As when her face is staind with magicke arts con-
> straint.   (vii.34)

The shield's exceeding brightness, which darkens even the sun and moon, recalls Lucifera's palace that dismays the "purest skye with brightnesse" (iv.4). Yet the new wording suggests not presumption but a power in fact greater than the most dazzling natural forces, a light brighter than pagan Phoebus and purer even than chaste Cynthia. Fashioned by Merlin, the magic of this shield is fundamentally different from Archimago's.

> No magicke arts hereof had any might,
> Nor bloudie wordes of bold Enchaunters call,
> But all that was not such, as seemd in sight,
> Before that shield did fade, and suddeine fall.
>   (vii.35)

Archimago's spells create deceiving images, but the shield possesses the power of truth.

After so many melancholy episodes, the very fact of Arthur's gay appearance is dramatic, and his arrival transforms the emotional atmosphere of the poem. In the remainder of the canto Una explains her plight and

Arthur sympathetically insists that she cheer up, reminding her that "Despaire breedes not . . . where faith is staid" (vii.41), a phrase that looks forward to the Despair episode in canto IX. Una tells her entire history—the recapitulation punctuates this turning point of Book One—and Arthur admits that her troubles could shake the stoutest heart. Nevertheless, she must take comfort in the knowledge that he will not forsake her until he has freed her knight. And, for the first time in the poem, Spenser concludes a canto on an unambiguously positive note: "His chearefull words reviv'd her chearelesse spright, / So forth they went, the Dwarfe them guiding ever right" (vii.52).

Canto VIII

The opening of canto VIII recalls the moment when Error wound Redcross in her train and Spenser called for God's help:

> Ay me, how many perils doe enfold
>> The righteous man, to make him daily fall?
>> Were not, that heavenly grace doth him uphold,
>> And stedfast truth acquite him out of all.
>> Her love is firme, her care continuall,
>> So oft as he through his owne foolish pride,
>> Or weaknesse is to sinfull bands made thrall:
>> Else should this Redcrosse knight in bands have dide,
> For whose deliverance she this Prince doth thither guide.   (viii.1)

Spenser's exclamation brings Arthur's role into abrupt focus, encouraging us to understand his rescue of Redcross in the action that follows as the intervention of "heavenly grace." True, and yet Arthur, a man with a human name and history, is not an allegorical figure like Error. We can perhaps say that providence is acting through Arthur, but it would be a mistake to hang a pasteboard label around his neck: Heavenly Grace. We should remember that Spenser's call in canto I did not produce direct divine intervention but that help did come in the form of Una's encouraging cry. The present situation is similar, and Redcross' need will again be providentially met, though not by direct divine intervention.

Arthur's fight with Orgoglio, the first episode, begins at the gates of the giant's castle with the trumpeting of a blast at which "every dore of freewill open flew" (viii.5). The grammatical ambiguity in "every dore of freewill" is telling: Redcross has been captured by a giant who is much like himself; he has yielded to the demands of his flesh, and before there can be any struggle, before the mortification of the flesh can begin, his will must be released from the prison it has constructed for itself. Furthermore, the blast recalls the trumpet flourish before Redcross' "apocalyptic" battle with Sansjoy, but this time the contest is a struggle between true opposites and the apocalyptic overtones are not ironic.

Orgoglio is a ponderous brute, Arthur the light-footed embodiment of chivalry. The battle is a struggle between savagery and civility, and Orgoglio's fleshiness, his clumsy weight—it may be suggestive to remember here that Spenser often uses "heavy" as a synonym for "sad"—is a major disadvantage. The giant seeks to kill Arthur with a single blow from his massive club, but the knight lightly dodges it and the stroke falls upon the ground with such force that the earth—one of the sources of Orgoglio's being, we remember—is badly wounded. Redcross, too, dodged the giant's club, only to be overthrown by the wind of the stroke, but Arthur has not been weakened as the young knight was. Spenser emphasizes Orgoglio's self-defeating nature here, comparing the stroke to a thunderbolt hurled by Jove to "wreake the guilt of mortall sins" (viii.9). Just as providence is operating through Arthur, so it is operating through Orgoglio, making him his own scourge. So deeply has the giant driven his club into the ground that he has trouble extracting it, and Arthur, perceiving his advantage, deftly slices off Orgoglio's arm. The first round is Arthur's, and in stanza 11 Spenser, reminding us of Orgoglio's fundamentally sexual nature, concludes it by humorously comparing the giant's cries of pain to an aroused herd of bulls bellowing in frustration at not being allowed to get at their cows.

Mounted on her seven-headed beast, Duessa tries to rescue Orgoglio but the prince's squire blocks her way until she enchants him, sprinkling magic poison on—again, the implications are sexual—"his weaker parts" (viii.14). Dismayed to see the young man into "such thraldome brought" (viii.15), Arthur rushes to his aid and cleaves one of the monster's heads. But now Orgoglio has revived and, joining the fray, delivers his second blow. Arthur is stronger than Redcross and fully armed besides; yet natural power, Spenser suggests, is finally insufficient to save one from Orgoglio, for the giant's second stroke throws Arthur to the ground: "What mortall wight could ever beare so monstrous blow?" (viii.18). Arthur, however, is not just a "mortall wight," for he possesses the miraculous diamond shield, a more than natural power, and in fact Orgoglio's second blow is as self-defeating as the first. The stroke fells Arthur, but in his fall the cover is ripped from his shield, releasing a dazzling light that renders the giant impotent. Again Spenser employs a lightning simile to suggest the operation of providence, this time comparing the shield's effect to "th'Almighties lightning brond," which "daunts the senses quight" (viii. 21).

The concept of daunting the senses, conquering the

flesh, is also perhaps implicit in Arthur's progressive, limb-by-limb dismemberment of the giant. Having dazed Orgoglio with the shield's light, Arthur cuts off the giant's leg, felling him like "an aged tree, / High growing on the top of rocky clift, / Whose hartstrings with keene steele nigh hewen be" (viii.22). In bringing down Orgoglio, Arthur is defeating the sensual world, the confusing world of appearances in which Redcross has gone astray, and it is appropriate that the giant's fall should be compared to a tree's, recalling the wandering wood and Fradubio's wooden prison. But the tree is only the first of two similes; Spenser goes on in stanza 23 to compare Orgoglio's fall to a castle's—the image recalls Lucifera's castle, founded upon the material world—"undermined from the lowest ground, / And her foundation forst, and feebled quight." The implications of Orgoglio's fall are enormous. Indeed his fall is so great that the entire natural world seems threatened: "Such was this Giaunts fall, that seemd to shake / The stedfast globe of earth, as it for feare did quake" (viii.23). But Spenser is careful to indicate that the earth only seems shaken, for nature is not evil, only limited. In fact the threat, as Spenser presents it, does not come from the physical world; rather, the danger lies in not perceiving nature's limits, not realizing the feebleness of the flesh either as a foundation for life or as an antagonist. And this of course is what Spenser, brilliantly employing the anatomical metaphor, suggests at the end of the fight when Arthur finds that the giant has vanished, "and of that monstrous mas / Was nothing left, but like an emptie bladder was" (viii.24).

Canto VIII consists of two segments, each 25 stanzas long. The first half describes Orgoglio's defeat and concludes with Duessa's thwarted escape. The second half, beginning with Una's formal expression of thanks to Arthur, describes Redcross' deliverance and Duessa's unmasking.

Accepting Una's thanks and entrusting Duessa to his squire, Arthur enters Orgoglio's castle, which turns out to be as weirdly empty as the giant himself. At last an "old old man" creeps forth, Ignaro—a personification of intellectual vacancy that complements the castle's physical emptiness—who gives the same reply to every question that Arthur asks: "He could not tell." No knowledge of religious history is necessary to appreciate the pathos of this silent castle and its feeble custodian, but it may be useful nonetheless to know that Spenser probably intends the castle, guarded by ignorance and dominated by the giant of fleshly delight, as an image of the Church on the eve of the Reformation.

Arthur discovers Redcross in the castle's dungeon, which is reached by a "deepe descent, as darke as hell" (viii.39), a phrase that associates Arthur's descent with the poem's earlier expeditions to the underworld, Archimago's embassy to Morpheus and, more important, Duessa's descent to the pagan nether regions with Night. Duessa's purpose was to assist a friend; carrying Sansjoy's broken body with her, she sought to cure him in the underworld. Arthur's descent, also undertaken to help a sick friend, is the Christian antithesis of Duessa's. His way of helping is to raise Redcross from the giant's "hell," from all those powers of darkness that the knight, who only peered a little way into the gloom of Error's cavern, has not understood.

The man that Arthur finds is a "ruefull spectacle of death" (viii.40), practically a corpse. In effect, Redcross has died:

> His sad dull eyes deepe sunck in hollow pits,
>   Could not endure th'unwonted sunne to view;
>   His bare thin cheekes for want of better bits,
>   And empty sides deceived of their dew,
>   Could make a stony hart his hap to rew;
>   His rawbone armes, whose mighty brawned bowrs
>   Were wont to rive steele plates, and helmets hew,
>   Were cleane consum'd, and all his vitall powres
> Decayd, and all his flesh shronk up like withered
>   flowres.   (viii.41)

In canto VII, at the start of the Orgoglio episode, Spenser showed Redcross feeding on the "cooling shade," and with such a diet it is not surprising that we find him starved, his flesh withered like flowers that have received neither sun nor refreshing water. Shocked by her knight's emaciation, Una asks how he came to be robbed of his "selfe." But, even as we sympathize with her dismay, Una's question reminds us of how unsatisfactory the young man's former self was. As I implied earlier, Arthur's fight with Orgoglio is concerned with the mortification—literally, the killing—of fleshly pride, the conquest of sensuality, and, sad as it is, the image of Redcross' decayed body perhaps also has a potentially positive aspect, representing a necessary preliminary to his reformation.

Canto VIII is a series of revelations about the nature of evil. In the first episode, Arthur exposed Orgoglio's emptiness; in the final one, he exposes Duessa, whose attractions are as illusory as the giant's power. Stripping away Duessa's royal robes, Arthur reveals her to be an old and loathsome hag:

> Her craftie head was altogether bald,
>> And as in hate of honorable eld,
>> Was overgrowne with scurfe and filthy scald;
>> Her teeth out of her rotten gummes were feld,
>> And her sowre breath abhominably smeld;
>> Her dried dugs, like bladders lacking wind,
>> Hong downe, and filthy matter from them weld;
>> Her wrizled skin as rough, as maple rind,
> So scabby was, that would have loathd all womankind.
>
> Her neather parts, the shame of all her kind,
>> My chaster Muse for shame doth blush to write;
>> But at her rompe she growing had behind
>> A foxes taile, with dong all fowly dight;
>> And eke her feete most monstrous were in sight;
>> For one of them was like an Eagles claw,
>> With griping talaunts armd to greedy fight,
>> The other like a Beares uneven paw:
> More ugly shape yet never living creature saw.
>
> (viii.47-48)

This extraordinary portrait is primarily designed to generate an emotional response, to provoke our revulsion, but we should not fail to note such reminiscences of earlier motifs as the bladderlike breasts and the maple-rind skin, recalling Fradubio as well as the maple of the catalogue of trees, and of course the monstrous feet suggest how Duessa's life rests upon bestiality.

"Amazd" by Duessa's deformity—the familiar pun on amazed has a new meaning, suggesting the incomprehensibility of evil—the knights allow her to flee to "the wastfull wildernesse," and the canto concludes with Una and her friends assuming control of the castle. This conclusion probably alludes to the Reformation, the purging of the Church, although its effectiveness as a climax does not depend upon our sharing Spenser's partisan religious position but simply upon having felt the power of his narrative. At last Una and Duessa's positions have been reversed. Now it is the witch who is cast out to wander, while the weary lady finally finds a civilized place to rest.

Canto IX

The opening stanza of canto IX picks up the note of fellowship and harmony with which canto VIII concluded, developing it into a general statement about noble minds and, more abstractly, about the relationship of the various virtues to each other:

> O goodly golden chaine, wherewith yfere
>   The vertues linked are in lovely wize:
>   And noble minds of yore allied were,
>   In brave poursuit of chevalrous emprize,
>   That none did others safety despize,
>   Nor aid envy to him, in need that stands,
>   But friendly each did others praise devize
>   How to advaunce with favourable hands,
> As this good Prince redeemd the Redcrosse knight
>   from bands.   (ix.1)

The stanza glances back to the events of canto VIII—significantly, Spenser uses the charged word "redeemd" to describe Arthur's rescue of Redcross—but also looks forward to this canto's major episode, the encounter with Despair in which Redcross, trying to aid a distressed knight, finds that he needs help himself.

Before Spenser gets to the Despair episode, however, he devotes some twenty stanzas to Arthur's history. This material, the story of Arthur's upbringing and, more important, of his love for the Fairy Queen, might have been presented when Spenser introduced Arthur in canto VII. Why has he chosen to place it here? The answer lies in the story itself, a tale of heroic faith. Arthur's quest for Gloriana—again Spenser builds his poem on the analogy between faith in love and religious faith—prepares us for the Despair episode, which is also concerned with hope and faith.

The crucial part of Arthur's narrative is his dream vision. One day, weary of his usual active life, the prince, who had always scorned love, dismounted from his "loftie steed" and lay down to sleep. "Every sence" was bathed in sleep, and the phrase suggests that the event about to occur is supersensual: Arthur's knowledge of Gloriana does not come through the senses. It seemed to him that a "royall Maid" lay down beside him.

> Most goodly glee and lovely blandishment
>> She to me made, and bad me love her deare,
>> For dearely sure her love was to me bent,
>> As when just time expired should appeare.
>> But whether dreames delude, or true it were,
>> Was never hart so ravisht with delight,
>> Ne living man like words did ever heare,
>> As she to me delivered all that night;
> And at her parting said, She Queene of Faeries hight.
>>>>>> (ix.14)

Arthur's dream recalls Redcross' erotic night in Archimago's hermitage, an episode we can now appreciate as a parody and prophecy of this genuine vision. The temptress appealed to Redcross' desire for immediate physical consummation, and, appropriately, he awakened to find the false Una physically present. The Fairy Queen, however, merely asks Arthur to have faith in her reality and in her love for him, and he awakes to find himself alone. Nevertheless, the grass is pressed down where he dreamed the lady lay—a sign upon which to base his faith. Arthur has vowed not to rest until he finds his lady; nine months he has sought her in vain, but he will not ''that vow unbind.''

The story of the dream is Arthur's final contribution to Book One; his last appearance is as an image of heroic faith. But before he rides off on his quest for his unseen lady, he exchanges gifts with Redcross. The prince gives a diamond box containing a magic liquid that ''any wound could heale incontinent.'' Redcross reciprocates with a ''booke, wherein his Saveours testament / Was writ with golden letters rich and brave'' (ix.19). It is appropriate that Redcross' gift should be the New Testament, for he is after all the champion of the Christian faith. But there is also an irony in the gift of Christ's words, for, as the encounter with Despair will show, Redcross does not yet appreciate the full extent of their power. He has looked into the dungeon of worldliness and has discovered the prison of fleshly pride, but he has not yet learned the power of words either for evil or for good. In the Despair episode this power will at last be brought home to him, when he comes dangerously close to death under the influence of an evil orator.

The Despair episode begins in stanza 21 with the sudden appearance of a fleeing knight, his eye ''backward cast,'' and his steed—here as elsewhere the symbol of his spirit—flying as if out of control. Redcross intercepts the knight and asks for his story, assuring him that ''no daunger now is nye'' (ix.26). But the young man's confidence should make us cautious; after the escape from the House of Pride, Redcross also felt secure. Perhaps his eye, too, is cast backward, seeing only past dangers, and perhaps in his enthusiasm to help, to be to Trevisan what Arthur was to him in the Orgoglio episode, Redcross' own spirit is flying "as he his bands had brast" (ix.21)

Trevisan tells a story about a friend, Sir Terwin, who loved a disdainful lady—that Despair's victim is a lover emphasizes the thematic connection with Arthur's refual to despair—and a wicked man called Despair that he and Terwin encountered, who with "wounding words" made his friend commit suicide. "God you never let his charmed speeches heare" (ix.30). Redcross is incredulous: "How may a man (said he) with idle speach / Be wonne, to spoile the Castle of his health?" (ix.31). Trevisan's answer recalls the disabling stream of canto VII and Error's coils; he describes how Despair's speech melts into his victim's hearts, robbing their power, and warns the knight not to test himself against his "guilefull traine." Redcross, however, vows to meet Despair and asks Trevisan "of grace" to guide him to the villain. Trevisan's reply repeats the important word as he agrees to "ride / Against my liking backe, to doe you grace" (ix.32). The term "grace," emphasized through repetition, means no more in context than courtesy, ordinary human generosity. Indeed, what is striking is how limited Redcross and Trevisan's understanding of grace is: Spenser has designed the colloquy to suggest in advance why Redcross is vulnerable to Despair.

The Despair episode is the climax of the sadness theme that has been prominent from the beginning of the poem, when Spenser described Redcross as "too

solemne sad.'' The setting for the encounter is appropriately cheerless, a "hollow cave" that is "Darke, dolefull, drearie, like a greedie grave" (ix.33), with a shriek-
ing owl on top and surrounded by images of blasted,
barren nature, "old stockes and stubs of trees, / Whereon nor fruit, nor leafe was ever seene" (ix.34). Once
again Redcross pokes into a "darkesome cave," naively
seeking out a danger for which he is not prepared. Has
the young man learned nothing since he first peered
into Error's cave? At this moment Redcross' quest looks
hopeless, but we, no less than the knight, must overcome despair.

Inside the cave is the "cursed man" himself, "Musing
full sadly in his sullein mind," a picture of cheerlessness
and mental disorder:

> His griesie lockes, long growen, and unbound,
> Disordred hong about his shoulders round,
> And hid his face; through which his hollow eyne
> Lookt deadly dull, and stared as astound;
> His raw-bone cheekes through penurie and pine,
> Were shronke into his jawes, as he did never dine.
>
> (ix.35)

Wretchedly emaciated, Despair looks not unlike Redcross when Arthur discovered him in Orgoglio's dungeon, for from one point of view Despair is an aspect of
Redcross. The picture reminds us that Redcross, too, is
still famished; he has been freed from fleshliness but has
not yet dined on truly nourishing food.

Seeing the corpse of Trevisan's friend, Redcross is
outraged: "With firie zeale he burnt in courage bold, /
Him to avenge, before his bloud were cold" (ix.37).

The young man now imagines himself an Arthur, and with a subtle change in wording Spenser repeats a phrase he applied to Arthur when he described the prince in search of Orgoglio's dungeon "with constant zeale, and courage bold" (viii.40). The changed wording, however, the substitution of "firie" for "constant" and the insertion of "burnt," transforms the phrase from a description of heroic determination to one of blazing passion which again evokes the presumptuous Phaethon. More important, Arthur's purpose was rescue, Redcross' is vengeance. Still unable to see beyond the sad old code of an eye for an eye—we remember the significance of the vengeance code in canto V, the fight with Sansjoy—Redcross angrily demands justice of Despair: "Thou damned wight, / The author of this fact, we here behold, / What justice can but judge against thee right, / With thine owne bloud to price his bloud, here shed in sight?" (ix.37). Ironically, the last line evokes not only the idea of vengeance but a very different mode of blood for blood: Christ's sacrifice, the realization of divine mercy for mankind.

Redcross' fundamental weakness, suggested by both his cheerless aspect and his undernourished condition, is his ignorance of God's love: he is still without faith. Having demanded justice, he has attacked in terms that make it easy for Despair to defend himself, and the villain parries Redcross' assault by throwing back the idea of justice with calm disdain: "What franticke fit (quoth he) hath thus distraught / Thee, foolish man, so rash a doome to give? / What justice ever other judgement taught, / But he should die, who merites not to live?" (ix.38).

Being concerned with words, this encounter is cast as a debate, a verbal battle. But in this warfare Redcross is clearly inferior, and Despair with his "wounding words" strikes most of the blows. In stanza 39 Despair argues that it was not only justice but "great grace"—he employs the word in precisely the limited sense that Redcross understands it—to help Terwin on his "wearie wandring way" to his "wished home." And in stanza 40 he turns from defense to assault, insisting that Redcross himself needs his aid:

> He there does now enjoy eternall rest
>> And happie ease, which thou doest want and crave,
>> And further from it daily wanderest:
>> What if some litle paine the passage have,
>> That makes fraile flesh to feare the bitter wave?
>> Is not short paine well borne, that brings long ease,
>> And layes the soule to sleepe in quiet grave?
>> Sleepe after toile, port after stormie seas,
> Ease after warre, death after life does greatly please.
>
> (ix.40)

In this stanza Despair's rhetoric has become hypnotically rhythmic, the slowly unfolding lines heavy with alliteration and, especially in the final sentence, long caesural pauses. But Despair's power is only partially a matter of rhythm and alliteration; his persuasiveness depends ultimately upon a certain truth in what he says, for he has tapped a powerful natural spring, the universal human longing for peace. Moreover, he has couched his appeal in a powerful metaphor: "port after stormie seas," after all, is what Spenser's poem is all about. Despair is so persuasive, his appeal so rooted in natural desire, that perhaps we miss the barb in the final line, the poisonously phrased sting in Error's tail: "death after life does greatly please." On the contrary, death never pleases; men naturally desire life. Despair's "guilefull traine" has led to a grossly unnatural conclusion.

Despair's assault surprises the young man, who for a moment stands silent, wondering at the villain's "suddeine wit." Then he replies that although life is limited a man has no right to commit suicide: "The souldier may not move from watchfull sted, / Nor leave his stand, untill his Captaine bed" (ix.41). Significantly, Redcross' simile derives from Cicero, a pagan philosopher, and Despair, whose own speeches are a pastiche of ancient sentiments, is easily able to counter by extending the simile, arguing at the end of the same stanza that the captain does permit his soldier to "depart at sound of morning droome." But in this rapid—and feeble—exchange, Despair has discovered the gap in Redcross' armor. Lacking faith and thus ultimately without hope for life, the knight has implicitly assented that death can be desirable.

And now, his opponent's vulnerability revealed, Despair presses for the kill with six stanzas of monologue aimed at Redcross' heart. In stanza 42 he develops Redcross' conception of the "Captaine" into an argument against free will, proving tht destiny is unavoidable. Then, in the following stanzas, he uses Redcross' own notion of justice to demonstrate the futility of his life, reminding him that he too has killed and "bloud must bloud repay" (ix.43). Again and again Redcross has failed, abandoning Una, defiling himself with Duessa, and winding up in Orgoglio's dungeon where, except for "lucke," he would have died. His life has been wretched, and why should he wish to prolong it? More important, he has proved his sinfulness and he himself knows the punishment for crime:

> Is not he just, that all this doth behold
>   From highest heaven, and beares an equall eye?
> Shall he thy sins up in his knowledge fold,
>   And guiltie be of thine impietie?
>   Is not his law, Let every sinner die:
> Die shall all flesh? what then must needs be donne,
>   Is it not better to doe willinglie,
>   Then linger, till the glasse be all out ronne?
> Death is the end of woes: die soone, O faeries sonne.
>   (ix.47)

Once again, Despair is persuasive not only because of the force of his rhetoric but because his arguments possess truth: Redcross *has* failed repeatedly. Nevertheless, Despair's understanding of the truth is limited, and Spenser has organized the long speech to expose him as well as to reveal his power. After all, it was not merely luck that Arthur was able to save Redcross: Una's love for her knight led Arthur to the dungeon. Heaven is just, as Despair maintains, but also loving and merciful. And, finally, at the climax of his speech Despair calls Redcross a "faeries sonne"—throughout *The Faerie Queene* Spenser preserves a distinction between the noble fairies, servants of a genuine but worldly glory, and the humans, who are Christian; we know that he is not a fairy but Saint George.

Redcross, however, does not know who he is, and for him Despair paints a plausible picture. Ironically, the preceding adventures in which Redcross has learned to see through appearances to the truth beneath—the dungeon of the House of Pride, the ugliness beneath Duessa's beauty—have made him even more vulnerable. The challenge to Redcross this time is to see beyond a limited truth to a higher one, and for this he is wholly unprepared. Understandably, then, Despair's words accomplish their deadly purpose as effectively as Archimago's charms did earlier:

> The knight was much enmoved with his speach,
>   That as a swords point through his hart did perse,
>   And in his conscience made a secret breach,
>   Well knowing true all, that he did reherse,
>   And to his fresh remembrance did reverse
>   The ugly vew of his deformed crimes,
>   That all his manly powres it did disperse,
>   As he were charmed with inchaunted rimes,
> That oftentimes he quakt, and fainted oftentimes.
>
> (ix.48)

Redcross has learned about depths but not about heights. Despair takes advantage of his incomplete knowledge, his readiness to believe in depths that are not immediately apparent, by showing him a picture of a dungeon even more horrible than Orgoglio's and no less true: hell.

> The sight whereof so throughly him dismaid,
>   That nought but death before his eyes he saw,
>   And ever burning wrath before him laid,
>   By righteous sentence of th'Almighties law. (ix.50)

Despair has won. A dis-made man, Redcross can see only death and punishment. But the victim must deliver the final blow himself, and for the coup de grace Despair places a dagger in his hand, which Spenser, re-

minding us of the fearfulness of one who has not trans-
cended nature, compares to a trembling aspen leaf.

Once again, as earlier when Redcross was wrapped in
Error's train and Spenser called for God's help, Una intervenes, snatching the knife from her lover's hand:

> . . . Fie, fie, faint harted knight,
> What meanest thou by this reprochfull strife?
> Is this the battell, which thou vauntst to fight
> With that fire-mouthed Dragon, horrible and bright?
>
> Come, come away, fraile, feeble, fleshly wight,
> Ne let vaine words bewitch thy manly hart,
> Ne divelish thoughts dismay thy constant spright.
> In heavenly mercies hast thou not a part?
> Why shouldst thou then despeire, that chosen art?
> Where justice growes, there grows eke greater grace,
> The which doth quench the brond of hellish smart,
> And that accurst hand-writing doth deface.
> Arise, Sir knight arise, and leave this cursed place.
>
> (ix.52-53)

Despair's logic has been tortuous, his rhetoric heavy, his
verses slow and lulling. Una's plain, staccato words ex-
plode like a flood of light, and Spenser describes their
effect on Redcross with conspicuous simplicity: ''So up
he rose, and thence amounted streight'' (ix.54).

The final image of the canto, however, is not simple
but grotesque. Left behind by Una and Redcross, the
villain tries to hang himself as he has vainly tried a thousand times before. But for him there can be no release
until Judgment Day, for, after all, his name is Despair.

Canto X

In canto X, in which Una brings him to the House of Holiness, Redcross adds faith to his force and discovers who he is. Having learned the power of words in his encounter with Despair, he is at last ready to receive the Word of God and become a Christian knight.

Spenser's style changes markedly in canto X. As in canto III, the pervasive irony disappears. There irony was replaced by elaborate rhetorical pathos, but here the verse becomes simple and straightforward with few flourishes or formal similes, a rhetorical change heralded by Una's plain speech at the end of the Despair episode. The narrative mode also changes as in canto X Spenser suddenly floods his poem with transparent allegorical figures such as Zeal, Reverence, Mercy, and Contemplation. In previous cantos the episodes tended to be complex in meaning and dependent upon multiple points of view; here, however, the concept of point of view hardly seems to apply, and meaning is as transparent as character. Moreover, Spenser's posture in the canto is at times conspicuously naive, as, for example, when he apologizes for not describing the New Jerusalem, ''Too high a ditty for my simple song'' (x. 55). Compared to earlier cantos, the simple allegory of the House of Holiness seems almost childlike, but this ostentatious simplicity in a canto devoted to truth is no less calculated than the earlier complexity in cantos concerned with error.

The opening stanza of canto X looks backward, asking us to reconsider Redcross' presumption in fighting Despair. Would he not have been a coward if he fled?

> What man is he, that boasts of fleshly might,
>   And vaine assurance of mortality,
>   Which all so soone, as it doth come to fight,
>   Against spirituall foes, yeelds by and by,
>   Or from the field most cowardly doth fly?
>   Ne let the man ascribe it to his skill,
>   That thorough grace hath gained victory.
>   If any strength we have, it is to ill,
> But all the good is Gods, both power and eke will.
>
> (x.1)

Before encountering Despair, Redcross assumed that his enemies were corporeal. His task was to prove his heroism by slaying such men as Sansfoy. Yet the deeper threat was never to the knight's person but to his spirit: the danger in the Sansfoy episode, for example, lay not so much in the Saracen's prowess as in his name. All Redcross' enemies have been words. Archimago, Duessa, Sansfoy, Lucifera, Sansjoy, Orgoglio—all are secret names that the knight was unable to read. Significantly, the last in the series of enemies, Despair, is a clear English word, the first since Error. Just as Despair's name is not disguised in a foreign language, so his threat is not disguised as corporeal power. Encountering him, Redcross in effect learns to ''read'' his foes. Or, to put it differently, he learns the real nature of his enemies, a discovery that Spenser confirms in the opening stanza of canto X by for the first time explicitly referring to ''spirituall foes.'' A man must not flee from spiritual foes, but neither can he overcome them without help; any spiritual strength that we have comes from God. Thus, in a simple statement of doctrine, these lines formulate what we and Redcross have learned about human weakness and prepare for a canto of explicit religious indoctrination.

Una brings Redcross to the House of Holiness as Duessa had brought him to the House of Pride; Una, however, is selflessly concerned for Redcross' health whereas Duessa was thinking only of her own weariness. Spenser has designed the two houses so that the contrast between them will be as striking as that between the ladies. We can hardly miss the significance of such details as the contrasting porters, Malvenù and Humiltá, or the difference between the broad highway leading to the one and the straight and narrow way into the other. But the contrast is not just a matter of detail; the houses are fundamentally different, and Spenser attempts to suggest this by radically changing his method of presentation. In introducing a materialist culture, Spenser relied, appropriately, upon physical appearances, giving us extended descriptions of the castle and Lucifera. In introducing the House of Holiness, on the other hand, he largely avoids describing appearances, giving us instead people in action. Spenser thus directs our responses in basic ways, implying that, whereas the House of Pride was ultimately an object, the House of Holiness is a genuine human community.

Beggar-my-neighbor was the rule in Lucifera's castle, a place of elaborate courtly ceremonies that did not hide the rapacious selfishness of both mistress and servants.

In presenting the inhabitants of the House of Holiness, Spenser stresses their simplicity and benevolent concern for each other and for their guests. Passing through the castle gate, Una and Redcross are met in stanza 6 by Zeal, a "francklin faire and free," who entertains them with "comely courteous glee" and "gladly" guides them to the hall. There Reverence, a gentle squire of "milde demeanure" and "rare courtesie," greets them with a modest welcoming speech and brings them to his mistress. These courteous gentlemen had no counterparts in the House of Pride; there, we remember, Redcross and his lady had to find their own way through a staring crowd to Lucifera, who greeted them from her throne with characteristic haughtiness. But Dame Caelia—her name means "heavenly"—is as warm and welcoming as Lucifera was icy.

Again and again Spenser emphasizes the calm happiness of the House of Holiness, and this of course is one of his principal points: here is a way of life fit for human beings, a civilization that brings joy rather than sadness and strife. After Redcross has been introduced to Caelia, her daughters, two "most goodly virgins" named Fidelia and Speranza, enter with arms affectionately linked, and Spenser briefly describes them in terms of a number of familiar symbols associated with Faith and Hope. Part of a trio of sisters that forms the Christian antithesis to the three Saracen brothers—Fidelia, like Sansfoy, is the eldest, for Faith leads to Hope and, finally, Charity—the ladies exchange "kind speeches" with Una, who learns that Charissa, the third sister, has lately given birth. And on this note of natural happiness the canto's first section concludes as Caelia, seeing that Redcross and Una are weary, sends them off to rest.

In the House of Pride Redcross stood still, spiritually halted, while the deadly sins jolted by. Now, after his rest, he is in steady movement, growing into understanding and health as he visits Fidelia, Speranza, Patience, and Charissa in turn. His first need is faith, which was inaccessible so long as he lacked even a rudimentary sense of spirit, but now he is prepared for Fidelia's schooling, ready to "heare the wisedome of her words divine" (x. 18). Like Archimago, Fidelia carries a book, and she too can rule the material world, commanding the sun, parting waters, and moving mountains. Led into faithlessness by Archimago's deadly words, Redcross is led into faith as Fidelia teaches him from her magic book truths beyond the reach of reason, initiating him into the higher mysteries of the spirit.

But the immediate effect of Fidelia's instruction is distressing. Recapitulating the Despair episode, Spenser tells us that at this point in his spiritual development Redcross becomes so conscious of his sinfulness that he wishes to "end his wretched dayes" (x. 21). Speranza teaches him to hope, but the knight's misery persists and at last a doctor, Patience, is called in. What is required, Patience realizes, is a physical cure, the mortification of the flesh. In a recapitulation of Redcross' starvation in Orgolio's dungeon, the doctor lodges his patient in a deep, dark place, dieting him strictly under the care of four nurses, Amendment, Penance, Remorse, and Repentance. Bizarre and painful as it is, Patience's treatment, which involves bleeding and the cutting away of flesh as well as flogging with a whip, has much in common with actual Elizabethan medical practices and should not be mistaken for punishment. Its result is to restore Redcross to health and thus make it possible for him to be introduced to the exuberantly healthy Charissa.

A joyful and vigorous mother, surrounded by babies—her brood is of course the antithesis of Error's—Charissa instructs Redcross in love for mankind, and so that he will better understand her teaching she entrusts him to Mercy, who introduces him to seven holy men. These seven men, the custodians of Charissa's charity hospital, correspond to the medieval *opera misericordiae,* the seven corporal works of mercy. But it is hardly necessary to be familiar with medieval doctrine to appreciate their selflessness and to realize that they represent the healthy antithesis to the diseased, solipsistic deadly sins of the House of Pride.

The visit to the hospital concludes the canto's central section, and, as at the end of the introductory section, Spenser punctuates the completion of Redcross' education in the active life of holiness by having him rest before proceeding. The canto's final section is concerned with the contemplative life. Even though Redcross has chosen the active life of a knight rather than the contemplative life of a thinker, he needs to understand what he is fighting for, and thus the natural completion of his education is a vision of the heavenly city.

Redcross' adventures in the House of Pride led ultimately to his discovery of the palace dungeon. His adventures in the House of Holiness lead toward heaven as, assisted by Mercy, the young man climbs the steep hill where the hermit Contemplation lives. Foreshadowed by the false hermit of canto I, Archimago, who dwelt down in a dale, Contemplation is a "godly aged Sire," who has mortified his flesh. In his emaciation Contemplation not only recalls Redcross after his experience in Orgoglio's dungeon—unlike the starved knight, however, Contemplation is full of "spirituall repast"—but also Despair, another, very different, guide to an eternal home.

Contemplation at first resents the visitors' intrusion—Archimago was suspiciously anxious to help his visitors—but Mercy persuades him to reveal the path to heaven and the old man, accordingly, leads the knight to the "highest Mount."

> Such one, as that same mighty man of God,
> That bloud-red billowes like a walled front
> On either side disparted with his rod,
> Till that his army dry-foot through them yod,
> Dwelt fortie dayes upon; where writ in stone
> With bloudy letters by the hand of God,
> The bitter doome of death and balefull mone
> He did receive, whiles flashing fire about him shone.
>
> Or like that sacred hill, whose head full hie,
> Adornd with fruitfull Olives all arownd,
> Is, as it were for endlesse memory
> Of that deare Lord, who oft thereon was fownd,
> For ever with a flowring girlond crownd:
> Or like that pleasaunt Mount, that is for ay
> Through famous Poets verse each where renownd,
> On which the thrise three learned Ladies play
> Their heavenly notes, and make full many a lovely
> lay. (x.53-54)

These are the first formal epic similes of the canto and, coming immediately before the climactic vision, they provide a dramatic pause. Each simile alludes to a mountain of divine inspiration: Mount Sinai, where Moses received the Ten Commandments; Jesus' Mount of Olives; and Mount Parnassus, in classical mythology the home of the nine muses. We should note how the reference in stanza 53 to Moses leading the Hebrews across the Red Sea from Egypt prepares for the movement from the stern first simile to the gentler image of the "deare Lord" on his fruitful hill. In progressing from the Old to the New Testament we are recapitulating the fruition of the Hebraic law in the promised land of Christian grace.

The third simile, however, initially seems misplaced, for according to the historical logic of progressive revelation the classical allusion ought to come first. Indeed, the very oddity of concluding the series in this way shifts our attention from the poem to the poet, encouraging us to realize that the chronological progression from the holy books to Mount Parnassus is strictly accurate: the story we are reading is neither the Old or New Testament but a poem that, like the final simile, emerges from them, combining their inspiration with that of the muses. Together the three similes describe the multiple nature of the mountain upon which Redcross must stand to see the New Jerusalem. In other words, they form the basis for his vision. Or, to apply the image to the poem itself, they suggest the triple basis of Spenser's authority for daring to describe the transcendent.

The description of the mountain is couched in the

high heroic style of formal epic, but when he confronts eternity, Spenser's style becomes conspicuously humble. In stanzas 55 and 56 Contemplation indicates the path, ''both steepe and long''

> Which to a goodly Citie led his vew;
> Whose wals and towres were builded high and
>   strong
> Of perle and precious stone, that earthly tong
> Cannot describe, nor wit of man can tell;
> Too high a ditty for my simple song;
> The Citie of the great king hight it well,
> Wherein eternall peace and happinesse doth dwell.
>
> As he thereon stood gazing, he might see
>   The blessed Angels to and fro descend
>   From highest heaven, in gladsome companee,
>   And with great joy into that Citie wend,
>   As commonly as friend does with his frend.
>
>   (x.55-56)

The abrupt shift in stylistic level is a brilliant rhetorical tactic: not only does Spenser suggest a height beyond the reach of the highest poetic style, he also conveys a sense of heaven as a wonderfully simple and informal place, majestic yet friendly. Heaven is the ultimate community.

Dazzled, Redcross realizes that the New Jerusalem is even more beautiful than Gloriana's city of Cleopolis, the capital of Fairy Land; and here Spenser indicates the relationship between the city of genuine worldly glory and the city of God. Contemplation reminds Redcross that ''for earthly frame'' Cleopolis is the ''fairest peece, that eye beholden can'' (x.59) and that it is proper for knights to serve Gloriana. Nevertheless, after he has won his ''famous victorie,'' Redcross should put earthly conquests behind him and make his pilgrimage to the New Jerusalem: ''For thou emongst those Saints, whom thou doest see, / Shalt be a Saint, and thine owne nations frend / And Patrone: thou Saint George shalt called bee'' (x.61). Cleopolis stands in much the same relation to the heavenly city as the Law does to Grace; service of Gloriana is a necessary step along Redcross' path, but ultimately even she must be left behind for a greater glory. Like the ''bloudy letters'' of the Law from the perspective of gentle Grace, even the victories achieved for Gloriana must, in the perspective of joyous heaven, seem sad and sinful, for ''bloud''—and by ''bloud'' Spenser means not only the bloodshed of battle but humanity itself—''can nought but sin, and wars but sorrowes yield'' (x.60). Hearing this, Redcross begs to be allowed to leave the world immediately, but the desire to escape the pain of the human condition is no less a temptation than Despair's. Contemplation has shown Redcross a way out of the world, but, unlike Despair who put the knife in his hand, he reproves him for thinking of abandoning his calling as a knight.

Contemplation has already mentioned Redcross' true name, but in his momentary desire to escape his destiny the young man ignored the revelation. Now, having accepted the burden of his fate, having discovered in the largest sense who he is, Redcross learns his name. Contemplation explains that Redcross is not an Elf, as he had supposed, but an Englishman brought up by a plowman in Fairy Land and given the humble name

Georgos—"farmer" in Greek—"Till prickt with courage, and thy forces pride, / To Faery court thou cam'st to seeke for fame, / And prove thy puissaunt armes" (x.66). From plowman to knight—the little history recapitulates the pattern of Redcross' experience in the House of Holiness in which nature has grown toward glory, and it reminds us, too, of Prince Arthur's knighthood, based upon a transformation rather than a rejection of nature. The name Georgos may also be meant to remind us of Vergil's *Georgics* and of his progress from the humbler forms of pastoral poetry to the epic glory of the *Aeneid*. And, in evoking Vergil, Spenser is perhaps reminding us as well of his own poetic growth from the pastoral *Shepheards Calender* to the heroic *Faerie Queene*, recalling how, as he put it in the proem, his "Muse whilome did maske . . .in lowly Shepheards weeds." The pattern of all great accomplishment is the same, Spenser would suggest, and he himself, writing of Saint George, is in a sense repeating his hero's history.

Redcross' path to heaven begins on earth, and therefore, thanking Contemplation, he looks back to the ground. At first he cannot see his way because his eyes are still dazzled by the brightness of heaven which did—the key phrase from the House of Pride recurs, transformed again—"too exceeding shine" (x.67). At last, however, "whenas himselfe he gan to find" (x.68), he returns to Una and together they set off to fight the dragon.

This canto begins abruptly. Instead of sliding into the action after a stanza or two of general reflection, Spenser starts the narrative immediately: "High time now gan it wex for Una faire, / To thinke of those her captive Parents deare, / And their forwasted kingdome to repaire" (xi.1). But Spenser's departure from his usual manner of beginning each canto is itself a kind of witty reflection of the conclusion of canto X in which Redcross overcame the temptation to escape from heroic action by indulging in prolonged contemplation.

In the first few stanzas Spenser arranges his characters for the battle before the prison of Una's parents, and then interrupts to invoke Calliope, the muse of heroic poetry. Coming at this point, the invocation emphasizes the battle's climactic importance. But it is, we should note, a rather peculiar invocation. Spenser asks the muse to come "gently," without "that mighty rage, / Wherewith the martiall troupes thou doest infest, / And harts of great Heroes doest enrage" (xi.6). The invocation is of course a classical convention, here strikingly transformed to apply to the gentle Christian hero, one who has put away rage. Spenser is reminding us that Redcross is a "man of God" (xi.7), and that the battle we are about to witness will be fundamentally different from the bloody triumphs of the ancient heroes.

The apocalyptic dragon fight, which occupies all of canto XI, takes three days, the period probably alluding to Christ's harrowing of hell between the crucifixion and the resurrection. Certainly, the dragon is meant to remind us of the dragon of the Book of Revelations, the "old serpent," Satan. Foreshadowed by Error, and indeed by all the evil figures, the dragon of canto XI is Redcross' ultimate antagonist, the summation of all ugliness and evil. In the course of fighting him, Redcross recapitulates his earlier adventures; Spenser means us to see that the knight has in effect been struggling with this dragon ever since the poem began. Lost as he may have seemed, we appreciate now that Redcross' entire career has been a fulfillment of his quest.

Spenser's description of the dragon's half-flying, half-running approach, like the description of Arthur's approach in canto VII, which it ironically recalls, occupies eight stanzas. Our initial impression of Arthur was of an approaching light. The dragon, "That with his largenesse measured much land, / And made wide shadow under his huge wast; / As mountaine doth the valley overcast" (xi.8), is an approaching mountain—an image that impressive though it is, reminds us of Fidelia's even more impressive power: "And eke huge mountaines from their native seat / She would commaund, themselves to beare away, / And throw in raging sea with roaring threat" (x.20). Arthur was armed from "top to toe," and so is the dragon, completely covered with "brasen scales" like a "plated coate of steele . . . That nought mote perce" (xi.9). Whereas Arthur's armor was for defense, the dragon quickly becomes an aggressive bird of prey, as Spenser compares his shaking scales to an eagle rousing his feathers upon spying a victim. The image of the eagle leads naturally to a description of the dragon's wings, which Spenser compares to sails, developing the simile into an extended image of the dragon as a ship—possibly an allusion to the Spanish Armada of 1588 and the sea battle that the Elizabethans considered an apocalypic contest between good and evil.

After providing the initial impression of Arthur, Spenser focused on his helmet, carrying our eye upward as he touched upon particular details. In describing the dragon, he also moves our eye upward in an ascent of progressively greater horror as he focuses upon each of the monster's weapons. Stanza 11 describes his tail. The great original of Error's tail and all the other winding, evil trains of the poem, the dragon's tail is coiled in "thicke entangled knots" with two stings—suggesting, perhaps, sin and death—both deadly sharp. But the dragon's claws, described in the first part of stanza 12, are even sharper than his stings. And most horrible of all is his mouth, gaping "like the griesly mouth of hell" (xi.12).

Spenser climaxed his presentation of Arthur with the description of his brilliant shield. The climax here is a description of the dragon's shieldlike eyes:

> His blazing eyes, like two bright shining shields,
>> Did burne with wrath, and sparkled living fire;
>> As two broad Beacons, set in open fields,
>> Send forth their flames farre off to every shire,
>> And warning give, that enemies conspire,
>> With fire and sword the region to invade;
>> So flam'd his eyne with rage and rancorous ire;

> But farre within, as in a hollow glade,
> Those glaring lampes were set, that made a dread-
>   full shade.   (xi.14)

Blazing with wrath like invaders' beacons—this simile
may be another allusion to the Armada—the flaming
eyes evoke the whole sad heroic code that Spenser's
poem repudiates, the ethic of fire and sword, vengeance
and destruction. And, in a grotesque parody of true joy,
the dragon gaily advances anticipating another victim,
"bounding on the brused gras, / As for great joyance of
his newcome guest" (xi.15).

On the first of his three days of fighting, Redcross
battles the dragon without magical assistance. His
efforts are heroic but, relying on native strength alone,
he gets the worst of the fight. In effect, Redcross fights
this day as a natural man, and to make this clear Spenser
designs the battle as an extended allusion to the
knight's adventures through canto IX, that is, to the
period before his introduction to Christianity in the
House of Holiness.

The first exchange may remind us in a general way of
the fight with Error, Redcross' first encounter with evil.
Redcross takes the initiative, but the knight's blow lands
"rudely"—the word suggests lack of skill as well as aggressive intent—and the dragon, like Error, overcomes
his enemy with his tail, knocking Redcross to the
ground. However, as in the earlier fight, the final blow
of the exchange is Redcross'. The knight rises—both
falling and rising are of course symbolic actions—and
delivers a stroke that impresses the monster: "For never

felt his imperceable brest / So wondrous force, from hand of living wight'' (xi.17). But, powerful as it is, the blow glances off the monster's hide.

After the fight with Error evil took the offensive as Archimago made Redcross fly from Una. In the second exchange here, which may be a witty allusion to that episode in a visual pun on ''fly,'' the dragon lifts both knight and horse into the air ''to beare them quite away'' (xi.18). The image of the knight's soaring perhaps also alludes to his stay at the lofty House of Pride. As Redcross escaped the usual fate of Lucifera's servants, so now his struggles impede the dragon's flight, forcing the monster to let him down ''before his flightes end'' (xi.19). Indeed, in this exchange he even manages to pierce the dragon's armor, wounding him under the wing.

After his escape from the House of Pride, we saw Redcross ''Pourd out in loosenesse'' (vii.7), drowning in sensuality with Duessa. In the dragon fight, too, his momentary triumph leads to a flood as the monster's wound releases a ''river of blacke goarie blood, / That drowned all the land, whereon he stood; / The stream thereof would drive a water-mill'' (xi.22). The casual reference to the mill, suggesting that a destructive force might be converted to drive an engine of civilization, is worth remarking because in it is implicit one of Spenser's most fundamental ideas—that great forces such as human sexuality are only good or evil according to use. Overcome by Orgoglio at the climax of his dalliance with Duessa, Redcross was of course defeated by his own pride. But we can perhaps see in Orgoglio himself only a savage and misdirected version of the same "forces pride" that originally, as Contemplation put it, impelled him to "seeke for fame" at Gloriana's court (x.66). In his early adventures Redcross' pride, his spirited and passionate nature, was both his strength and his weakness. This was implicit in the opening image of his horse straining at the bit, and now Spenser makes the idea explicit as the emblems of Redcross' knighthood, his horse and armor, contribute to his downfall.

In stanza 23 the dragon hurls his tail around Redcross' steed, who gets so entangled that he throws his master to the ground. Fallen, the knight strikes a futile blow and becomes "wroth"—a quasi-symbolic word, suggesting that his spirit is betraying him. The dragon replies with a fiery blast that burns the knight's beard, symbol of his manliness, scorches his face, and, worst of all, heats his steel armor so that which "erst him goodly arm'd, now most of all him harm'd" (xi.27). Redcross' torment in the burning armor not only suggests the betrayal of his heroic spirit in yielding to passion, but also implies how all that this particular armor represents has become unbearable to his flesh. Earlier, we remember, Redcross withdrew from the scorching heat of the sun, and in canto VII, yielding to erotic passion, he removed his armor, thus leaving himself vulnerable to Orgoglio. But now, though he longs to throw his armor off, he bears the heat heroically, and Spenser compares his agony to that of Hercules—as a pagan hero Hercules is an appropriate figure to evoke on the first day of Redcross' fight—when he put on the burning shirt of Nessus.

Redcross agony recalls the mortification of his flesh in Orgoglio's dungeon, just as his longing for death in stanza 28 echoes the Despair episode that immediately followed. Una's love prevented the knight's suicide, and now again Redcross escapes death through love: God's love for man, revealed through grace. Overthrown by a final blow from the dragon's tail, as in canto IX he was overthrown by Despair's "guilefull traine," Redcross falls into the miraculous "well of life," full of "great vertues,"

> For unto life the dead it could restore,
>   And guilt of sinfull crimes cleane wash away,
>   Those that with sicknesse were infected sore,
>   It could recure, and aged long decay
>   Renew, as one were borne that very day.
>   Both Silo this, and Jordan did excell,
>   And th'English Bath, and eke the german Spau,
>   Ne can Cephise, nor Hebrus match this well;
> Into the same the knight backe overthrowen, fell.
>
> (xi.30)

We should note the emphatic position of the key word "fell" at the end of the episode's final stanza. But although Redcross, like every son of Adam, has fallen, his is a fortunate fall. This is the magic well prophesied by Fradubio, the water that frees one from imprisonment in nature. Redcross' restorative night in the well, symbol of baptism, corresponds to his initiation into Christianity in the House of Holiness.

In stanza 31 Spenser describes the day's end in mythological terms as, like Redcross, the blazing sun sinks into water:

> Now gan the golden Phoebus for to steepe

> His fierie face in billowes of the west,
> And his faint steeds watred in Ocean deepe,
> Whiles from their journall labours they did rest.
>
> (xi.31)

This image reaches back to the very beginning of the poem when, arguing by analogy to the sun that at night ''doth baite his steedes the Ocean waves emong'' (i.32), Una advised Redcross to rest. The young man's watery night in Archimago's hermitage, bathing in erotic fantasies, was a parodic prophecy of his rest in the true house of religion and of this magical night of immersion.

Una spends the night in watchful prayer for her champion until, like a favorable omen, the sun rises from the sea with a ''deawy face'' (xi.33). Immediately, Redcross leaps from the well, not only refreshed—as he never was at Archimago's hermitage—but completely new-made:

> As Eagle fresh out of the Ocean wave,
> Where he hath left his plumes all hoary gray,
> And deckt himselfe with feathers youthly gay,
> Like Eyas hauke up mounts unto the skies,
> His newly budded pineons to assay,
> And marveiles at himselfe, still as he flies:
> So new this new-borne knight to battell new did rise.
>
> (xi.34)

Before the first day's fight Spenser compared the dragon to an eagle, and in stanza 19 to a hawk; now the fight is to be more equal, for, magically transformed by the well, Redcross has also become a bird of prey.

The knight begins the second day's battle with a blow

to his enemy's head, and this time his sword pierces to the dragon's skull. In stanza 36 Spenser calls our attention to Redcross' new strength, explaining that he is unsure whether the stroke's success is due to some improvement in the sword or in the knight as a result of his baptism. (Both explanations are correct, for as a Christian Redcross himself is stronger and wields a more powerful weapon against evil.) Enraged by the wound, the dragon roars like a "hundred ramping Lions" whom "ravenous hunger did thereto constraine" (xi.37). This image of ferocious, aroused nature—from the beginning Spenser has used the lion as a symbol of nature in both its positive and negative aspects—reminds us that in battling the dragon Redcross is in effect battling his own ravenous appetites, all the corruption of his physical nature, and it also prepares us for the dragon's fierce onslaught.

Redcross' opening blow is a prologue to the battle proper. Now the dragon takes the offensive and in three distinct attacks employs each of his three weapons in turn—tail, claws, and mouth. He strikes so hard with his tail that the sting pierces the knight's shield and lodges in his shoulder, "Where fast it stucke, ne would there out be got" (xi.38). But though he cannot remove the barb, cannot free himself entirely from the weakness of nature, Redcross is able to save his life and wound the dragon at the same time. Swinging his blade, he strikes powerfully enough to cut through the knotty tail: "Five joints thereof he hewd"—the number probably alludes to the five senses, which Redcross has learned to control—"and but the stump him left" (xi.39). The dragon's first attack suggests an assault upon the soul through the senses; the second perhaps suggests an assault through the intellect, the challenge of doubt to the shield of faith. The dragon siezes Redcross' shield in his claw, and, once again, although unable to remove the monster's weapon, the knight cuts himself free, leaving the claw hanging on his shield.

Redcross' weakness in the first day's fight lay in his passionate nature, his fiery spirit , and, significantly, the dragon defeated him with the blast of fire that prepared for a knockdown blow from the tail. Now, furious at having been twice thwarted, the dragon again blasts Redcross, the fire bursting out as "burning Aetna from his boiling stew / Doth belch out flames" (xi.44). The volcano simile, developing Spenser's initial comparison of the dragon to a mountain and also continuing the motif of eating and appetite, is an image of nature in eruption. But Redcross has learned the danger of the dragon's fire, and this time he avoids being enveloped in flame by retreating, stepping a "little backward for his best defence, / To save his bodie from the scorching fire" (xi.45). Redcross is not used to retreating, however; his heroic spirit has always advanced and sought out the enemy, even when such action was foolish. Again his passion to be the perfect hero, never daunted, never withdrawing, trips him up. Wearied and "with dread of shame sore terrifide" (xi.45)—fearful that his retreat is somehow shameful—the knight slips and falls in the mire.

Again Redcross' fall is fortunate. In this place there is a magic tree loaded with red fruit and producing a balm, which "overflowed all the fertill plaine, / As it had deawed bene with timely raine" (xi.48). We should note Spenser's emphasis on the color of the fruit, for this is not only the first tree of life from which Adam was excluded for his sin, but also the rood tree, the cross, with its red fruit—Christ's blood. The stream of balm, the antithesis of the overflowing Nile which it recalls, is another image of Christ's blood:

> Life and long health that gratious ointment gave,
> And deadly woundes could heale, and reare againe
> The senselesse corse appointed for the grave,
> Into that same he fell: which did from death him
>   save.   (xi.48)

As Redcross' second fight suggests, even a Christian falls repeatedly in the struggle against Satan and, to preserve life, more than baptism into the faith is required. All his life, Spenser seems to imply, the Christian needs to draw upon the miracle of Christ's power. Moreover, through that power, the Christian, weak and human though he is, will ultimately triumph; on the third day Redcross will kill the dragon.

The dragon fight is not only the image of the struggles of an individual soul but a mirror of mankind's historical development from a pre-Christian state. On the first day, before his baptism, the knight was no match for the dragon. On the second, after his introduction to Christianity, he was able to hold his own until he became tired and slipped. On the third, he kills the dragon. But this, historically speaking, is an event that will not occur until Judgment Day, when, according to Christian prophecy, Christ will at last triumph over the "old serpent.''Necessarily, then, in the transition between the second and third days, Spenser's story becomes a metaphor of apocalypse. In slaying the dragon, Redcross ceases to be a questing soul and becomes the perfected knight, becomes, in other words, an image of Christ himself triumphing over Satan.

Perhaps the most striking aspect of the final fight is its brevity. So long anticipated, the whole episode takes a mere five stanzas and the fight itself only one. The brevity is part of Spenser's point. Against absolute power there is no struggle; the dragon is overthrown in an instant. "The joyous day gan early to appeare" (xi.51), Spenser says, introducing the battle with a characteristically light touch, for if this is *the* "joyous day" it has indeed come early. In stanza 52 the knight leaps up freshly, and in stanza 53 the dragon charges with mouth gaping wide:

> He thought attonce him to have swallowd quight,
> And rusht upon him with outragious pride;
> Who him r'encountring fierce, as hauke in flight,
> Perforce rebutted backe. The weapon bright
> Taking advantage of his open jaw,
> Ran through his mouth with so importune might,
> That deepe emperst his darksome hollow maw,
> And back retird, his life bloud forth with all did
> draw   (xi.53)

Redcross slays the dragon by plunging to the pit of his maw, the "griesly mouth of hell" that is the original of all the earlier dark caves and also the source of all the poem's dangerous, enchanting words.

"So downe he fell": Spenser repeats this phrase four

times in stanza 54, the repetition emphasizing the magnitude and finality of the event. And then, in the canto's last stanza, Una confirms Redcross' victory, praising God and thanking ''her faithfull knight, / That had atchiev'd so great a conquest by his might'' (xi.55). By whose might? Does ''his'' refer to God or Redcross? Appropriately, this final line is completely ambiguous.

Canto XII

The country Redcross has liberated is Eden. By slaying the dragon he has reversed the consequences of the Fall, recovering the happy garden of man's golden age—except that Spenser's Eden is not a garden. The movement of his poem has been from isolation to community, from lonely struggle in savage surroundings to joyous civilization, and thus he boldly transforms the traditional pastoral paradise into a populous city, ruled by a king and queen. The analogy between Spenser and Vergil, implicit ever since the imitation of the *Aeneid* in the proem, is now complete: like Aeneas, refounding Troy in Latium, Spenser's hero has reestablished a famous city.

Eden in Spenser's vision is a strikingly warm and friendly place, dignified but unpretentious. It reminds us of the heavenly city of canto X, and, indeed, Spenser's rhetorical strategy in presenting Eden is an expanded version of the abrupt stylistic shift from the heroic description of Contemplation's mountain to the humble style of the transcendent vision. Canto XI, the winning of Eden in the dragon fight, is written in a high heroic style charged with allusion and complexity. Canto XII is much simpler, and again Spenser draws attention to his style, apologizing for not being able to describe Una adequately: ''My ragged rimes are all too rude and bace, / Her heavenly lineaments for to enchace'' (xii.23).

Throughout the poem Spenser has kept his role
conspicuous by interjecting personal reactions to events.
Implicitly, the poet himself has been a principal character, and, as in the case of other major figures, Spenser
has given himself parodic antitypes: Archimago, the
framer of hellish verses, and the time-serving
entertainers of Lucifera's court. Spenser's manner is
generally humble as befits a Christian poet, but his role
is heroic, for he too, in a sense, has been tracking down
the old serpent. Earlier Spenser hinted at the analogy
between his growth as a poet and Redcross' development from plowman to knight. Now, at the start of the
final canto, the analogy between the poet's quest and
the hero's becomes explicit as Spenser describes his
labors in the same sea-journey metaphor he has
repeatedly applied to Redcross:

> Behold I see the haven nigh at hand,
>> To which I meane my wearie course to bend;
>> Vere the maine shete, and beare up with the land,
>> The which afore is fairely to be kend,
>> And seemeth safe from stormes, that may offend;
>> There this faire virgin wearie of her way
>> Must landed be, now at her journeyes end:
>> There eke my feeble barke a while may stay,
> Till merry wind and weather call her thence away.
>>>>> (xii.1

Implicit in this opening emphasis on seeing, and in
the cautious "seemeth safe from stormes," is a
reminder of the poem's first lesson about recognizing
the limits of vision: appearances must be tested. This
theme provides the link with the action proper, which
begins in stanza 2 with the watchman spying the rising

smoke that "did seeme" to indicate the dragon's death. The watchman reports the news to the king, who is dubious. But this time, astonishing as they are, appearances are not misleading and, proving the report "true by triall" (xii.3), the king proclaims universal rejoicing. "Then gan triumphant Trompets sound on hie" (xii.4), Spenser says, reminding us of the false Judgment Day trumpets that blew at Redcross' tournament with Sansjoy. And at last, in an episode that has overtones both of Christ's release of Satan's prisoners in the harrowing-of-hell story and of the raising of the dead at the last judgment, the imprisoned population of Eden emerges from the castle. Redcross has finally proved an Arthur, releasing this nation from bondage as the prince had released him.

Stanza's 5-11 describe the procession from the castle to Redcross. Spenser uses this procession to control our emotional response to the victory, starting with solemnity that modulates into joy and finally becomes the homely comedy of the peasants. First he describes the king and queen, surrounded by their "sage and sober Peres, all gravely"—a pun suggesting resurrection—"gownd" (xii.5). Next comes a band of young men bearing laurel branches as tokens of victory and peace. (In the line of march the young men precede the royal group, but Spenser's description follows an emotional logic that reshapes the natural order of the marchers.) Next are the virgins, bearing garlands and timbrels, and then the "fry of children young," singing and playing with "childish mirth" (xii.7). Finally, even more childlike and comic than the children, according

to the aristocratic canons of Spenser's age, come the
"raskall many," the peasants who, in an affectionate
burlesque of the theme of not trusting appearances, are
described as warning one another that the dragon may
not really be dead. The procession concludes on a
domestic note—Spenser's images of joy and goodness
are often homely and domestic—with a peasant mother,
"Halfe dead through feare," telling her gossips how her
foolish son tried to play with the dragon's talons: "How
can I tell, but that his talents may / Yet scratch my
sonne, or rend his tender hand?" (xii.11).

One detail of the description I have not yet
mentioned. Spenser's verbal portrait has much in common with Renaissance painting, which abounds in
representations of processions, often with an important
symbolic figure or group in the center of the panel. The
imprisoning castle stands at one side of Spenser's large
picture and Redcross at the other—the dragon, interest-
ingly, cannot be located precisely, being somewhere in
the general background— but placed in the middle as a
central emblem of the whole is an image of triumphant
beauty and truth that seems to allude to Spenser's own
Queen Elizabeth: Una, "Who in her selfe-resemblance
well beseene, / Did seeme such, as she was, a goodly
maiden Queene" (xii.8).

After the procession, the king leads the way to the
palace for a simple feast where he hears the long story of
Redcross' misadventures and then addresses the knight:

> Deare Sonne, great beene the evils, which ye bore
> From first to last in your late enterprise,
> That I note, whether praise, or pitty more:

> For never living man, I weene, so sore
> In sea of deadly daungers was distrest;
> But since now safe ye seised have the shore,
> And well arrived are, (high God be blest)
> Let us devize of ease and everlasting rest. (xii.17)

From the beginning we have had an ironic perspective on Redcross, knowing more about him than he has. The king's speech summarizes our present understanding of the knight's situation: after troubled seas and danger of drowning, he has at last reached port. But Redcross corrects the king—and, implicitly, corrects us as well—revealing that he cannot stay in Eden but must return to serve the Fairy Queen. For the first time in the poem, Redcross' knowledge is greater than ours, and this change is an index of his growth.

Redcross' revelation returns the poem to history. Once again, as in the Sansfoy episode in canto II, Spenser is playing upon our response to allegory as a literary mode, but this time he is indicating our limitations rather than the knight's. The dragon fight and the ensuing celebrations in Eden have drawn us so far into an allegorical reading of these events as an image of the last judgment and the ultimate defeat of evil that, in our anticipation of the "joyous day," we have forgotten the literal level of the story in which the dragon after all is only a dragon and Redcross, brave as he is, still a knight. Our situation as readers is analogous to Redcross' on the mountain when he wished to anticipate the joyous day of his entry into the New Jerusalem. Contemplation directed him back to earth, and now the knight in effect leads us back to earth, reminding us

that a heroic life must be a continual quest. Redcross still
has six years—Spenser probably intends six, one less
than the sabbath number, to symbolize the whole term
of life—to serve the Fairy Queen in "warlike wize"
(xii.18).

The king of Eden has proclaimed that whoever kills
the dragon shall marry his daughter and inherit his
kingdom—inheriting a kingdom is a familiar romance
reward which here has obvious biblical overtones. Still
bound to Gloriana, Redcross must for a time put off his
marriage and his ultimate destiny as a prince in
paradise. Nevertheless, as a pledge of faith on his part
and love on Una's, the two are now formally betrothed.

The betrothal ceremony begins in stanzas 21-23 in
which the king summons the bride, "The fairest Un' his
onely daughter deare, / His onely daughter, and his
onely heire" (xii.21). The rhythmic repetition of
"onely," an allusion to Una's name, launches the poem
into the appropriate ritual mode for the ceremony and
also gives us an impression of the bride's stately,
measured steps as she solemnly advances. In two lovely
similes Spenser compares Una to the morning star,
herald of day, and to a spring flower, another harbinger
of joy. Then the promised light and joy burst forth:

> The blazing brightnesse of her beauties beame,
> And glorious light of her sunshiny face
> To tell, were as to strive against the streame.
> My ragged rimes are all too rude and bace,
> Her heavenly lineaments for to enchace.
> Ne wonder; for her owne deare loved knight,
> All were she daily with himselfe in place,
> Did wonder much at her celestiall sight:
> Oft had he seene her faire, but never so faire dight.
>   (xii.23)

The lines remind us of Lucifera's blazing. But whereas the false virgin queen's brilliance was associated with gorgeous clothes and jewels, Una wears the simplest of gowns, "All lilly white, withoutten spot, or pride" (xii.22). Lucifera's brightness was borrowed from material things; Una's is her own.

The betrothal ceremony proceeds into stanza 24 when, in the middle of the stanza, just as the king is about to address his daughter, a sudden interruption occurs. "With flying speede, and seeming great pretence, / Came running in, much like a man dismaid, / A Messenger with letters, which his message said." Spenser's abrupt return to the punning, ironic language of earlier parts of the poem—"pretence" in this context means "importance," but the word's usual sense is clearly intended as well, and "dismaid" is also a pun—puts us immediately on guard: whoever this messenger is, he bodes ill. The messenger's dramatic appearance is not unlike the interruption of a wedding that is always possible when the minister calls upon anyone who knows an impediment to speak or forever hold his peace. I suppose that at this point in a wedding nearly everyone, despite the best wishes in the world for the bride and groom, secretly hopes to hear someone raise an objection, and it is precisely upon this love of melodrama that here, as elsewhere, Spenser relies.

The messenger does raise a serious objection. He bears a letter from "Fidessa" claiming that Redcross is already betrothed:

> To me sad maid, or rather widow sad,
>> He was affiaunced long time before,
>> And sacred pledges he both gave, and had,
>> False erraunt knight, infamous, and forswore:

> Witnesse the burning Altars, which he swore,
> And guiltie heavens of his bold perjury,
> Which though he hath polluted oft of yore,
> Yet I to them for judgement just do fly,
> And them conjure t'avenge this shamefull injury.
>
> (xii.27)

Fidessa presents herself as "sad" because she has been abandoned, but her insistence upon her legal rights and her demand for vengeance are "sad" in another sense, reminding us of the gloomy world of the pre-Christian ethic which Redcross has indeed abandoned. (For simplicity's sake, Spenser does not distinguish between the pagan revenge code and the Hebraic code of law.)

Fidessa's demanding of rights is, we can note, very similar to Shylock's demanding his bond in *The Merchant of Venice*, a play that, like Spenser's poem, is concerned with law and grace, with Hebraic and Christian ethics. Portia defeats Shylock by turning the law back on him, warning that, although the bond permits him a pound of flesh, it nowhere allows him to shed a drop of Antonio's blood. Redcross, however, rejects the final authority of strict law. He acknowledges the bond but explains that there were extenuating circumstances, revealing that the woman is really Duessa and that he was deceived by witchcraft. He appeals to the king's mercy, appeals from the old dispensation to the new.

Redcross has exposed "Fidessa"—again, he has proved himself an Arthur, "stripping" the witch as the prince did in canto VIII—and now Una joins her knight in his plea, exposing the messenger as Archimago. The last half of canto XII parallels the last half of canto I.

Once again Archimago has disguised himself and attempted to come between Redcross and Una with words, the "bitter biting words" (xii.29) of law. But this time he is exposed, and Redcross and Una defeat the effort with words that are more powerful than his. "Greatly moved at her speach" (xii.35), the king commands that Archimago be imprisoned and the interrupted ceremony is resumed.

Redcross' dream of love in canto I concluded with a fantasy of a marriage feast in which "the Graces seemed all to sing, / *Hymen io Hymen*, dauncing all around" (i.48). Canto XII concludes with a nuptial celebration that is not a fantasy. With his "owne two hands" the king ties the "holy knots" (xii.37), bonds that are the joyous antithesis of Error's knots, and then the happy feasting begins, accompanied by both earthly and heavenly music. "Great joy was made that day of young and old," and Redcross himself is a "thrise happy man," for each time he looks at Una his "heart did seeme to melt in pleasures manifold" (xii.40). The image of his heart melting alludes again to that false dream of love when his "manly hart did melt away, / Bathed in wanton blis and wicked joy" (i.47) and to his long watery affair with Duessa. But this time, although "swimming in that sea of blisfull joy," Spenser assures us that

He nought forgot, how he whilome had sworne,
In case he could that monstrous beast destroy,
Unto his Farie Queene backe to returne:
The which he shortly did, and Una left to mourne.
(xii.41)

Our last image of Una recalls our first, when Spenser described her as "one that inly mournd" (i.4). Spenser's poem has come full circle: Redcross will begin another quest and again Una is in mourning. But the young man is now a proven knight, and Una, although parted from her betrothed, knows that the six years of their separation—besides symbolizing the term of life, the number also suggests the entire history of the world, thought to be six thousand years from creation to judgment day— will ultimately have an end.

The final stanza of canto XII also comes full circle as Spenser returns to the ship metaphor of the opening:

> Now strike your sailes ye jolly Mariners,
>   For we be come unto a quiet rode,
>   Where we must land some of our passengers,
>   And light this wearie vessell of her lode.
>   Here she a while may make her safe abode,
>   Till she repaired have her tackles spent,
>   And wants supplide. And then againe abroad
>   On the long voyage whereto she is bent:
> Well may she speede and fairely finish her intent.
>
> (xii.42)

In the opening stanza Spenser presented himself as analogous to Redcross; here he addresses us directly as "jolly Mariners." We too have been heroic voyagers, participating in the knight's quest. After our labors we may rest awhile in harbor, but, like Redcross' journey through life, at the end of Book One our epic voyage through *The Faerie Queene* has only begun.

Selected Bibliography

Editions

There are many adequate reading editions of Book One, but the standard reference edition is Frederick Morgan Padelford's volume in *The Spenser Variorum* (Baltimore: Johns Hopkins Press, 1932). Although somewhat dated, the *Variorum* contains a wealth of still useful information. An excellent annotated text edition of Books One and Two has been prepared by Robert Kellogg and Oliver Steele (New York: Odyssey Press, 1965). An annotated edition of the entire *Faerie Queene,* ed. A. C. Hamilton, will be published in the Longmans Annotated English Poets series.

Books

Alpers, Paul J. *The Poetry of "The Faerie Queene."* Princeton: Princeton University Press, 1967. An important book on Spenser's style with an excellent chapter on "Heroism and Human Strength in Book I."

Cheney, Donald. *Spenser's Image of Nature: Wild Man and Shepherd in "The Faerie Queene."* New Haven: Yale University Press, 1966. Ch. 1, "Plowman and Knight: The Hero's Dual Identity," is one of the best recent discussions of Book One.

Fowler, Alastair. *Spenser and the Numbers of Time.* London: Routledge & Kegan Paul, 1964. Numerological and astrological symbolism.

Hamilton, A. C. *The Structure of Allegory in "The Faerie Queene."* Oxford: The Clarendon Press, 1961. Ch. 1 is an excellent discussion of how to read Spenser illustrated with an analysis of the opening episode of Book One; ch. 2 also deals largely with Book One.

Hankins, John Erskine. *Source and Meaning in Spenser's Allegory: A Study of "The Faerie Queene."* Oxford: The Clarendon Press, 1971. Ch. 5 is useful in connection with biblical allusions in Book One; ch. 10 deals with historical allegory in Book One.

Hough, Graham. *A Preface to "The Faerie Queene."* London: Gerald Duckworth and Co., 1962. Useful background material on the Renaissance epic and a brief chapter on Book One.

Lewis, C. S. *The Allegory of Love.* London: Oxford University Press, 1936. A classic; the section on Spenser is still an excellent starting point for critical reading.

———*Spenser's Images of Life*, ed. Alastair Fowler. Cambridge: Cambridge University Press, 1967. Posthumously published lectures.

Nelson, William. *The Poetry of Edmund Spenser: A Study.* New York: Columbia University Press, 1963. An important general study with a chapter on Book One.

Waters, D. Douglas. *Duessa as Theological Satire.* Columbia: University of Missouri Press, 1970. Book One in connection with certain aspects of Protestant thought.

Williams, Kathleen. *Spenser's Faerie Queene: The World of Glass.* London: Routledge & Kegan Paul, 1966. An important general study with a chapter on Book One.

Articles

Anderson, Judith. "Redcrosse and the Descent into Hell," *ELH,* XXXVI (1969), 470-492.

———"The July Eclogue and the House of Holiness: Perspective in Spenser," *Studies in English Literature,* X (1970), 17-32.

Berger, Harry, Jr. "Spenser's *Faerie Queene,* Book I: Prelude to Interpretation," *Southern Review,* II (1966), 18-49.

Craig, Martha. "The Secret Wit of Spenser's Language," in *Elizabethan Poetry: Modern Essays in Criticism,* ed. Paul Alpers. New York: Oxford University Press, 1967.

Doyle, Charles Clay. "Smoke and Fire: Spenser's Counter-Proverb," *Proverbium,* XVIII (1972), 683-685.

Heninger, S. K., Jr. "The Orgoglio Episode in *The Faerie Queene,"* *ELH,* XXVI (1959), 171-187.

Kaske, Carol V. "The Dragon's Spark and Sting and the Structure of Red Cross' Dragon-Fight: *The Faerie Queene,* I.xi-xii," *Studies in Philology,* LXVI (1969), 609-639.

Kennedy, William J. "Rhetoric, Allegory, and Dramatic

Modality in Spenser's Fradubio Episode," *English Literary Renaissance*, III (1973), 351-368.

Kermode, Frank. *"The Faerie Queene*, I and V," in *Shakespeare, Spenser, Donne*. New York: The Viking Press, 1971.

Miller, Lewis H., Jr. "The Ironic Mode in Books I and II of *The Faerie Queene*," *Papers on Language and Literature*, VII (1971), 133-149.

Neill, Kerby. "The Degradation of the Red Cross Knight," *ELH*, XIX (1952), 173-190.

Orange, Linwood E. "Sensual Beauty in Book I of *The Faerie Queene*," *Journal of English and Germanic Philology*, LXI (1962), 555-561.

Schroeder, John W. "Spenser's Erotic Drama: The Orgoglio Episode," *ELH*, XXIX (1962), 140-159.

Sirluck, Ernest. "A Note on the Rhetoric of Spenser's 'Despair,' " *Modern Philology*, XLVII (1949), 8-11.

Weiner, Andrew D. " 'Fierce warres and faithful loves': Pattern as Structure in Book I of *The Faerie Queene*," *Huntington Library Quarterly*, XXXVII (1973), 33-57.

Whitaker, Virgil K. "The Theological Structure of *The Faerie Queene*, Book I," *ELH*, XIX (1952), 151-164.

Woodhouse, A. S. P. "Nature and Grace in *The Faerie Queene*," *ELH*, XVI (1949), 194-228.

DATE DUE

MAR 04 1988			
NOV 16 1991			